Skyline
2016

Cyberworld Publishing

www.CyberworldPublishing.com

Cyberworld Publishing
Jindalee St
Toronto, NSW, 2283
Australia

Skyline
2016

*An Anthology of
Prose and Poetry by
Central Virginia Writers*

Olivia Stowe, ed.

Table of Contents

Poetry

Prose Nonfiction

On Writing/Publishing

Introduction

Skyline 2016, the third in a series of annual publisher's anthologies produced by Cyberworld Publishing, showcases the prose and poetry talents of Central Virginia writers. The title of the anthology is taken from the Skyline Drive, the parkway skipping along the top of the Blue Ridge Mountains in Virginia and providing centering for the region in which the authors showcased here are living and writing. Thus far the editions have followed the seasons in cover image, with this being the spring edition.

There is no overarching theme for the works in this anthology, so each can be discovered and appreciated on its own context and merits. Over half of the works found here are works by Central Virginia writers that won or placed in various Virginia regional and statewide writing contests during 2014 and 2015. The foundation for the juried selection of contest selections consists of the 2015 writing contest of the Blue Ridge Writers Chapter of the Virginia Writers Club, a 2015 *Skyline* spring writing contest, the 2014 Writer's Eye contest of the University of Virginia's Fralin art museum, and the 2015 poetry awards of the Poetry Society of Virginia. Also included in the anthology are other works selected from the portfolios of these contest selectees, and special contributor works by established writers in the region. The judges, established writers all, of the 2015 *Skyline* spring writing contest were also invited to contribute.

The anthology consists of forty-seven works by twenty-three authors in four sections: fiction, poetry, nonfiction, and, since this is a writer's anthology, a section on writing and publishing. Eclectic is the hallmark word for this collection. Most of the authors here are purposely represented by more than one work and in varied media to showcase their writing skills. Notable among the contest-placing authors represented this year is Erin Newton Wells, who swept the placements in all contests represented here, including the annual Poetry Society of Virginia awards (although none of her winning poems from this last category are included in Skyline 2016).

The fifteen-story fiction section leads off with a story, "Invisible Women" by Leone Ciporin, that placed in one of the last John Grisham–judged runnings of the annual short story contest conducted by *The HooK*, a Charlottesville weekly that no longer is being published. Other stories provided by established writers include those of novelist and *Skyline* spring contest judge, Sarah Collins Honenberger, humorist Deborah M. Prum, and frequent short story contest winner Jody Hobbs Hesler. Poet and essayist Lauvonda Lynn M. Young's poetry leads off the seventeen-poem poetry section. The highly eclectic eleven-works nonfiction section is led off by a reflection of recent U.S. congressional election candidate Jack Trammell on being thrust into the national spotlight when his congressional campaign suddenly became key to the 2014 U.S. Congress elections. Essayist Susan M. Lanterman treats readers to the search for hidden treasures in the Victorian mansion she renovated into a Charlottesville B&B, and clinical psychologist Phyllis Koch-Sheras introduces readers to connection with their waking life through dreams.

In the four-essay "On Writing/Publishing" section, perhaps unique to this anthology, established writers Jody Hobbs Hesler, Sarah Collins Honenberger, *Skyline* spring contest poetry judge Lori Dixon, and Gary D. Kessler offer insights into various aspects of writing and publishing.

A notable additional section to this anthology is the "About the Authors" section, which provides fascinating, I think, literary background notes on the authors represented in this collection as well as the judges for the 2015 Skyline spring contest: Sarah Collins Honenberger for fiction, Lori Dixon for poetry, and Becky Mushko for nonfiction. Be sure not to miss the extensive and rich writing experience of our authors. I'm sure you will be as impressed with their accomplishments as I have been.

As with the initial *Skyline 2014* and *2015* editions, it has been a delight to work with and read the many varied themes and high quality of writing of these Central Virginia writers. I hope you will find these works as fresh and as entertaining and thought provoking as I have. These indeed are exceptional writers who deserve to have their works highlighted and represented in the marketplace.

Olivia Stowe
Volume Editor
Skyline 2016

PROSE FICTION

Invisible Women

Leone Ciporin

(Third place, *The HooK* fiction contest, and published in *The HooK*, 2012)

People notice dead women. After the third one, the Philadelphia media started lovingly resurrecting family backgrounds, social lives, and charitable causes, packaged in news shows like made-for-TV movies. As I snaked my way through our office cafeteria, the television on the wall blared a eulogy of the latest victim: "Miranda volunteered at a local homeless shelter every Sunday afternoon. As the shelter director said, 'she always thought of others first.'" The victim's face filled the screen, a happy brunette, her wide grin revealing healthy gums.

All the women were slim. And brunette. When I was little, my mother told me my hair was dirty blonde, like my father's. I'd wash it twice a day.

The woman in front of me in the entrée line lunged to rescue a fork falling through the slats holding her tray. She'd need to let a few more forks go before she'd fit the victim profile.

"Go ahead," I told a skinny man who bumped into me at the soft drink dispenser. I paid for my lunch and joined Lucinda at her table. We both worked as clerks at a Center City Philadelphia accounting firm. Our cubicles had faced each other until the office gods moved her three cubes away.

"Pretty scary." She tilted her head toward the television.

"Yeah. Neither of us has to worry, though," I said. Lucinda was in her sixties, with yellowy white hair and glasses. She considered contact lenses vain.

"Well, I don't." She sipped her ice tea. "But you, you're young and pretty. You should be careful."

I moved my peas away from my potatoes. "No need to worry about me. I'm invisible."

Lucinda warmed the inside of my elbow with thick fingers. "Oh, stop it, Amy! You're a sweet, pretty girl."

Apparently, the guys at McDougal's at happy hour that Friday didn't think so. I'd walked the few blocks from my office to the bar, surrounded by pulsating music from car radios and prolonged honking that passed for conversation between drivers. The city hummed louder on Fridays. Its narrow streets and wide sidewalks struggled to hold the crowd and I tucked in behind a man speaking at auctioneer speed into his cell phone. His wake cleared all obstacles except one Revolutionary War reenactor who'd wandered from Independence Hall. I detected the scent of mothballs as I evaded him.

Despite the gathering outside, McDougal's still offered pockets of air, its peak occupancy yet to come. I snagged a wobbly stool at the end of the bar and ordered a frozen margarita. The late June sun pushed in through tall windows, brightening the bar but melting the ice in my margarita. Global warming in a glass.

The shirt of the man next to me had a triangle of sweat pointing toward the middle of his back. His front poured charm at the woman sitting on his other side. She formed the center of a storm of men, of which he was merely a gust. In the mirror behind the bar, I watched her brush dark hair from her face before wrapping slender fingers around the stem of a white wine glass. Her tiny nose crinkled in laughter at some witty male comment.

Her nose looked flatter in the newspaper Monday morning. Victim Number 4. "The body of Betty Vanderkamp, 32, a breast cancer survivor, was found yesterday . . ." I pictured the men circling her that evening. Then Lucinda stopped by my cubicle for our break and I put the paper down.

"New picture." Lucinda pointed to the photo propped next to my mouse pad. Inside a cherry frame, my mother stood on her concrete steps, the white spiraled metal on her screen door partly visible. Her hand saluted to shield her eyes from the sun and her flowered dress fluttered away on one side, as if the breeze were reaching out to grab her.

My mother had never liked my job. She called it low status, like my father. My half-sister, Camille, had been an officer at a local bank. My mother often said Camille resembled her father, too. Jack, my mother's only husband. His pictures had stood on my mother's mantel and bedroom dresser. Curly black hair, freckles sprinkled over a wide face, uneven grin. My father appeared shortly after Jack's death, taking advantage of my mother's grief. He'd stayed just long enough to leave me as a souvenir.

I had a childhood picture of me with Camille, half of me hidden behind her. Our faces, both round, smiled. But the real reminder of my childhood appeared in my car window every day as I passed a playground on my drive home from the train station. Just before I crested the hill, the tip of the burgundy monkey bars would tantalize me. When my car reached the top and tilted downward, the hill acted as stadium seating for the playground scene.

My fondness for monkey bars came from my childhood walks to the playground. My mother and Camille would lope ahead of me, Camille's ponytail swinging side to side. I trotted behind with Fredo, a dog who'd wandered into our small yard one day and never left. At five, my head barely reached my mother's hip or Camille's ten-year-old shoulder. But being small put me closer to Fredo. He'd march next to me, tapping his wet, rough nose into the cradle of my palm. I'd wipe my hand dry by smoothing the white flyaway fur on his head. Though Camille asserted ownership as the first-born, Fredo and I knew he belonged to me. As soon as Camille left for college, I was allowed to have him in my room at night.

Once we reached the playground, my mother would deposit me in the sandbox with the toddlers while she went to the swings with Camille. She looked only at Camille, so I'd shake sand from my legs and run to the monkey bars, where I'd arm crawl across while Fredo leapt to nudge my heels along.

Maybe Camille loved those afternoons, too. Maybe that's why she bought a townhouse near a playground. I lived there now, having inherited it by default, along with all her personal belongings. Her favorite black dress, her pearl earrings, even the insulin for the diabetes she'd hated anyone knowing about.

My mother and Camille had been driving to brunch when a moving van punched a hole in their car. Camille, in the passenger seat, was killed instantly, but my mother lingered several days. I sat by her hospital bed constantly. For the first time ever, she'd focused on me, smiled at me, even stroked my hair with the scrap of strength she had left. I gripped her hand for hours, our fingers intertwining, and told her how much I loved her. The soft heel of her hand caressed my chin. She looked at me, only me, and I became real. Even the nurses paid attention to me, updating me on her condition and asking how I was feeling. Then she died and I became invisible again.

But Lucinda saw me. She brought me casseroles after the accident, patted my back when I cried in my cubicle, ate lunch with me. And now she'd invited me to visit the art museum with her, to see the newly expanded Impressionist exhibit. As a museum member, she had free tickets. She and her late husband had often walked there from their Center City condo, bought before downtown became upscale.

There were several restaurants near the museum and the café where we met for drinks played up its proximity by sprinkling Van Gogh and Renoir posters along its walls and giving some of its drinks cutesy names. I ordered a frozen Monet Mocha. Lucinda ordered ice tea.

I reached across her to pay for both drinks. She stuck her worn wallet between me and the boy at the cash register. "Let me get this," she said. "You shouldn't be paying for me."

I pushed her wallet away. "I owe you a lot more than a cup of tea."

"No, you don't, sweetheart. You've been through so much." But she tucked her wallet inside a crocheted handbag. We claimed two stuffed armchairs just as a family vacated them. We sat and I wrapped my hands around the glass and leaned over to take in the smell of cocoa.

After we climbed the steep museum steps, the hot atmosphere settled even more heavily on my shoulders, so I welcomed the goose bumps the icy lobby air brought. The bright colors worn by people filing into the Impressionist exhibit stood out against the tan and cream walls.

"I hate crowds." I pointed to the people bunching in front of two Monets, the tops of their heads seeming to float amid the water lilies. "Let's go to another room first." We headed toward lesser-known artists, our sneakers squeaking on polished floors.

I stopped in the middle of a rectangular room and leaned in toward a small painting before backing away to sit on a leather bench directly across from it. "I like this one." I pointed to the watercolor depicting a field in mid-harvest. At the field's far end, a woman with a basket stared out at us.

Lucinda strode up to the painting. "Why this one?"

"I like the woman at the edge." I leaned around the backpacks of a whispering couple who had stopped suddenly. "You have to see it from back here." Up close, the woman became blobs of chestnut hair, cream skin, and light-blue dress. But from afar, she looked right into you.

We passed through the museum store on our way out, browsing masterpieces that had been miniaturized and captured in refrigerator magnets and postcards. Lucinda picked out a book on the Impressionists and got in line.

A steady flow of customers kept both cashiers busy, with a man at one register periodically trotting over to help a trainee work the other register. "Joleen, remember to close the cash drawer after each sale."

Lucinda handed the girl her book and said, "I like your name."

"Perkins?" The girl looked at her nametag. "Oh, you mean Joleen! Thanks." She took Lucinda's credit card. "That book looks good. I keep meaning to read books like that, but running after a toddler—she wears me out. If my cousin didn't help, I'd be exhausted."

Lucinda said, "I saw a children's art book in that aisle." She pointed. "Maybe you and your daughter could read it together."

"Good idea." She slipped Lucinda's book into a plastic bag stamped with the museum logo and handed it to her with a smile.

Lucinda leaned in to whisper, "You're doing a good job." The smile widened.

Sunday evening offered perfect weather for weeding the small bed in front of my townhouse. A slight breeze lifted mildly humid air, helping the lowering sun ease up on the heat.

As I put on my gardening gloves, my neighbor pulled into his driveway and waved. "How's the bike?" He'd helped me fix my sister's mountain bike, inflating tires, lubricating gears. I still hadn't ridden it.

"Great! Thanks again for your help." I waved a gloved hand slightly before crouching back down and spotting a nasty spreading weed marring the bed. My fingers yanked it out. No matter how many times I pulled them out, the weeds always came back. The sun rubbed my back as my hands cleared the dark mulch. By the time I finished, despite a relatively cool summer evening, sweat had bloomed on my face and arms. I wiped my forehead with the sleeve of my shirt and headed in for a quick shower.

After combing my wet hair, I made myself a salami sandwich, the bread crumbs contaminating one of Camille's blue and white plates, and settled on the couch to watch the news. The fifth victim took the top story spot. "Joleen Perkins, twenty-eight, was found dead in her home early this afternoon. A single mother, she'd dropped her daughter off with a relative before going away overnight. When she didn't pick up her daughter this morning, the cousin went to her house and made the gruesome discovery. Police now suspect that the killings are caused by a massive overdose of insulin, probably administered by injection."

Talk of the killings rustled through the break room Monday morning. "Did you hear?" A plump woman handed me the powdered creamer. "They got the guy." The police were talking to a former boyfriend of one of the victims. He'd worked in the same building as another victim. The women in the office relaxed with an impromptu pizza party at lunch. I ate my two slices, but said nothing.

Two weeks later, the cafeteria television broadcast the news that the man had been cleared, even as they informed the city of the sixth victim. I felt relieved that he'd been let go. I didn't want an innocent man to suffer. I didn't want anyone to suffer. I just wanted to be visible, the way I'd been with my mother at the end, the way I was with Lucinda, and sometimes when someone first learned about the accident. But another Camille could eclipse me at any moment.

My teeth crunched on a piece of ice, but stopped mid-bite at the next comment in the news story. The ice melted on my tongue as the announcer said: "A neighbor called police when the woman's small dog wouldn't stop barking."

The dog would quiver at the front door tonight, waiting for the sound of her shoes, for the joy of a reunion that would never come. My throat let out a whimper for him. And for me. As soon as the Camilles went away, I could stop. Plenty of places they could live in peace. How much longer would it take?

I spotted Lucinda's head bobbing up and down near the cash register. Motioning her over to my table, I smiled to distract her from the tears in my eyes.

Rituals

Sarah Collins Honenberger

With one eye open above the microscope, Doctor Adrian Farandini squeezes the other eye shut. Alone in the laboratory, he perches above the small cone of light, his forehead slick with perspiration. In his head the memory of his grandmother's voice croons, gruff with old-country manners and yeast bread and Montepulciano's finest Valpolicella.

"Adi, sit down for a bit, and I'll tell you about the crazy goat we had when I was little girl."

He thinks, "Not now, Nonna. I'm busy, too busy for silly stories from a world that's gone."

Over the stainless steel echo of the high-ceilinged room he pulls the equipment closer across the black marble countertop. He shakes his head to clear the ghosts. On clean white graph paper he records his findings, precise letters on narrow black lines. A shrug to stiff shoulders, he marks a black star next to Slide 7482. On the same line he writes, "Check Tier 1, Reed."

The slides of leukemia patients who did not survive frame an internal landscape that never leaves him. He's spent his life searching for a link, a coincidence too coincidental to be meaningless. Dedicated, singularly focused, he's never asked to see the bodies preserved in frozen suspension, never met the families left behind. The job keeps him late. At home his wife entertains herself with foreign movies, expensive lingerie, and Chinese food. Vaguely he recalls, whenever he's home in time to kiss her good night, that before the banns were announced they violated their Roman Catholic upbringing more than once. Lately, though, it's hard for him to remember why. While she spends mornings in the city arranging charity bazaars, she's always home for after-school snacks, soccer practices, and Girl Scouts on alternate Thursdays. His children do not wait up.

Activating the microscope's inner camera, he studies the endlessly fascinating circular world of disease and dysfunction. He labels each miniature photograph. After he selects another slide from the tray, he replaces the last in its appointed slot. Repetition means certainty. Certainty saves lives.

Pleased at his progress, he smiles to the naked rows of beakers in full military array. They are steadfast companions, never departing for fancier jobs with better pay and fewer hours. Examine, compare, record, examine, compare, record: protocol dictates. The grandmother who leans heavily over his shoulder, her garlic breath sweet and discomforting, he ignores.

"Adi, you're missing your daughter's ballet recital. Your son needs help with algebra. I cannot tell for sure about your wife, but, if you don't listen, she won't be your wife much longer."

"Go away. Distraction makes me sloppy, Nonna. If this research fails, children around the globe will die. The enemy will win. Leave me alone."

At midnight he washes his hands with bacteria-resistant soap. The neon germs slide into the drain, gone before he can catalogue the day's results. He trails his own monotone hum of satisfaction as he strides to the cafeteria. Bagel and jasmine tea, he loads the tray without noticing the mesmerizing pattern of marbleized swirl in the stagnant water of the egg warmer. The room is full of tables. Four equidistant chairs flank each polished square of Formica, an unthinking regiment of islands in a foreign sea. Although money clinks in the register's return, Doctor Farandini hears nothing.

"Good evening, Doctor. Don't forget your change," the attendant says. A baby-faced girl, barely tall enough to reach the register keys, she looks away as he passes without speaking. He is not shocked by her tongue ring or the cobra tattoo that stretches across one naked forearm to lunge at the soft untanned skin on the other side. He's still quantifying slides, considering, deliberating.

He takes three cream cheese packets, but pushes them under the napkin when he recalls how loudly his wife announces the damage to his heart every morning at breakfast. So coldly she speaks, her lips jammed tightly against each other, pale and bloodless in irritation, as if the effort is not worth it, not at all the way he remembers his grandmother's affectionate lilt.

"Why don't you have an orange, Adi? I taught you better than that. An orange a day . . ."

"It's apples, Nonna, an apple a day. But I'm allergic to Vitamin C. Don't you remember when I was five?" In their imaginary conversation his own smile rises unbidden. His eyes flash back and forth across the deserted room. He is unable to choose a table for the distraction of his grandmother standing close.

"You fed me Sicilian oranges," he whispers. "At the market. But walking back to the villa, I threw up on that dusty road. Spitting, choking. You can't have forgotten?" The boy remembers it all. Afterward the priest came, his bare ankles below his cassock as he sat the donkey. With smooth uncalloused hands, he pilfered olives by the handful and urinated on the grapevines, the donkey abandoned at the top of the hill. And he lowered his hands in the open cistern and tried to scrub away the proof.

"Is that what convinced you to dedicate your life to fighting germs, my serious Americano grandson?"

There is no answer in the deserted cafeteria. No one understands, yet she asks because she's entitled to ask, his elder. He has never gone back to the villa. Not when his parents grew weary of American ways and moved back, one terse good-bye to their only son, the great doctor, and barely a letter since. Not when Nonna begged him to bring the first great-grandson to be baptized in the true church. Not even when she died. From his entire forty-six years this single regret he holds closest to his heart. He's never gone home.

Perhaps he should go now, visit her grave, stay at the villa one more time with its tangy smell of grapes ripening in the sun, steam rising from the large copper pot of pasta pulled and palmed on her worn dark hands, cool tiles on his bare feet. Then put it behind him, once and for all. Cleansed and redeemed, he could return and finish his life's work, unlock the secret of the microscope's vision.

For a long time the doctor thinks about the last time he sat on his grandmother's lap. The dirt and orange pulp mixing in thick puddles, the feel of the earth so close that you could lie

24

down and sink into the dust, a flounder on the ocean bottom, camouflaged, safe.

An edge of hillside hugs the villa wall. Hemp-toned stucco climbs to red-tiled roof. Indigo clumps of lavender cling to the stones along the road and silvery rosemary sheaths open their arms in greeting. The sun, a giant orb ringed with streaks of tangerine, rust and gold, floats on gilded waves.

He had cried out, "Nonna. Nonna. Come see the paint God spilled on your sky."

Scooping him up, she pressed him against her wide bosom, drank in his fragrance and whispered Italian words that tickled. Some of her in him, there in her villa, she loved him because they shared the painted sky.

"How will He clean it all up, Nonna?"

No answer but the aria—strange, foreign words of love and longing, duty and disappointment—and his legs swung out from her belly as she twirled and dipped in the dripping paint of the Italian day. When she set him down on the cracked dry earth, he wept that it ended so soon. An ancient little man even then, and wise.

If he were to sign out from the lab and the institute, call his wife, buy tickets, fly over the ocean to a country he hardly remembers and a graveyard full of people for whom he's never had time, he might miss the single slide that links the rest.

"*Ah, but you may already have missed it, Adi,*" his grandmother insists, "*with your tired eyes and bent back, just as you've missed the ballet and the baseball. Go home.*"

In that single instant Doctor Farandini's dull brown eyes grow wide. His heart misses a beat, four, seven. He gasps, reaches for the table edge. Third generation to ancestors long dead, six feet below the earth that encircles the long-ago villa, he pushes away the vision, remembers instead what waits in the laboratory upstairs. He rises, shoves away the uneaten food, decides not to wait for the elevator. On the stairs he berates himself for letting fantasies delay the real work of posterity. On each landing he pauses to restore a prescribed oxygen level.

If his heart gives out, heaven knows his proper wife will grieve. She will orchestrate the funeral, walk hand in hand with their blue-eyed children to the grave. Crying neatly into her monogrammed handkerchief, she will cross fingers to chest in cautious obedience to the memory of rituals long abandoned. Afterward, with the children secured inside the limousine, she will receive neighbors and scientists, doctors and lawyers, and even the stockbroker who may hold her hand after the others depart.

To Doctor Farandini, with each step on industrial linoleum the scene grinds away from comfort. By the fifth landing he feels how much thinner the air is.

"Foolish boy, old age should come easily, not panting and breathless in the stale recycled air of a ten-story building. Let the young ones take charge," his grandmother mutters in Italian.

His breath labored, his heart numb, he closes his eyes. Across the far ocean a breeze lifts the olive branches, a lazy signal of welcome and abandon. Her bent fingers peel the tangerine skin off the sweet moon of dripping fruit. The petals fall. Dark stains of Sicilian juice spread down her dress, her grandmother's flowered dress. Drying in the Italian sun, the stains fade to stiff peach icicles on the threadbare cotton.

She holds his hand—the boy again—and he leans over the ditch. Tugging his sandaled toes back from the ridge, she wipes his chin. She chuckles at the grandson greedy for the fruit, unschooled, ignorant of consequences and effects.

"Don't run, silly child," she scolds. *"Home is just ahead. Soon enough the breeze and the well water will ease your fever."*

"I see it," he cries out. "There, at the curve, beyond the tallest cedar. Let me go."

Yet, when he reaches the top floor, there is the familiar hallway. He sinks his shoulder against the fire door. He tramps past doorway after doorway to the laboratory until his palm rests against the cold, metal handle. On the other side of the glass the lights gleam above his work station. Within the florescent brightness the instrument bulb drains to a concentric circle of pale light, a halo above the microscope. The long-ago aria rises up to greet him.

"Isn't it beautiful, Nonna?" But the handle sticks, refuses to open. He rattles it, blinks, tries again, pounds on the door. Glaring down the empty hallway, he fumes, furious at the

26

new paint, the printed restrictions to avoid any hint of contagion. He rails at lazy colleagues in starched lab coats who ignore the trays of waiting slides, who drink coffee, and talk baseball scores while children die.

Doctor Farandini refuses to recant. He marches along the lab wall and peers into the dusky chamber. Through bumpy glass the lab coats hang useless on metal hooks. Fourth from the end, the pocket of his own coat bulges with his keys. Although he knows the guard locks the door when the last doctor departs, Doctor Farandini tries it anyway, the last doctor but one. At the knob's unforgiving pressure, he leans against the wall, his stomach twisting with the late dinner. He sinks to the floor.

In his ear his grandmother whistles. *"It's alright, Adi, come back tomorrow. No more today, a blessing. Go home to your boy, your girl, your wife who may not be your wife if you don't."*

"I could do two more trays, perhaps three."

"Never mind, sweet boy."

He thinks of the villa and the sun-soaked dusty road under the painted sky. Perhaps she is right. He should go home, pat his children's heads in sleep, and lie next to his wife, rest, dream. In the elevator his fingers shake as he tucks in his shirt, fuzzy reflections in the chrome stretch his head, draw out hollow cheeks and thinning hair. A stranger stares back at him. At the ground floor the elevator jerks and bounces ever so slightly and he is the doctor again, slight and stooped.

Under the streetlamps the parking deck glows alien green. At the car he fumbles in his pockets. Everything is in his lab coat, locked upstairs. He will walk. He knows the way. Yet the soles of his black wingtips are too thin for slick pavement or vineyard paths. His steps echo, just enough human noise that the dream and the villa fade. Block after block, the buildings fall away. Dark unformed space loiters between the last gas station and his intermittent shadow. He passes a school, perhaps where his children study while he works in the lab. He's not sure.

Years ago he recalls a Sunday afternoon, two, of frenetic racing between slide and swings. This may be the place. The past looms like a mugger, poised to steal what it can.

Yes, Doctor Farandini is convinced this is the place. He sees the bench where he sat while they shrieked and ran. He read the advance sheets from research institutes he can still recite by heart; each one associated with a colleague whose work he admires. The dates, the discoveries, each with its own importance in a parade of knowledge that is his life. No one can deny it. He has made contributions of significance. His careful records, the slides, the photographs, enough reward.

"Go on, go on, silly boy. You'll catch cold in the damp air."

At the playground's edge she beams encouragement. Her one gold tooth glints in the headlights of a passing car. How different life would have been there without steel boundaries and ninety-degree walls.

At the edge of the woods a car is parked, not quite hidden under the maple overhang. His heart races. He worries over the wide black stretch of sidewalk before the far streetlight. He walks faster.

Closer, and the windows are fogged over. Blurred shapes rise to their own flowing rhythm, slowly, smoothly. He slows too, moving still, but unable to look away. Between clouds, the moonlight exposes shapes that melt together, move in tandem, shapes and spaces, spaces and shapes, intimate and revealed. A single hand presses against the glass, the fingers taut and spread. Beyond, in the darker void, a bare shoulder crests and sinks. The windows steam, the images erased.

Doctor Farandini's breath bleats out. Anxious, surprised, he sucks in night air and hurries forward, past. A new memory materializes. Perspiration melts into sweet perfume, fingertips play lightly on pale skin, muscles twist to cross a warm leg, a palm curves into taut thigh. His wife, a long-ago smile.

And then he is safe, beyond the car, back in the visionless night. The car a car again, anonymous and mundane where pavement grinds out to dirt. A streetlight burns just short of the parking lot. Yet he forces himself to walk, the steps counted out loud, no longer measuring distance. His shoes are too tight. They pinch his toes and rub his heels where he is not accustomed to walking. Around his collar exertion clings, damp and embarrassed.

He tries to call up the memory of the Mediterranean sun that warmed him as a boy. He concentrates and there is Nonna, astride the ridge to catch her breath. He runs to her, circles around her, and she draws him close.

"Stop, boastful boy, stop and look on the earth and sky that made you who you are."

The forgotten lavender and gold swirl around him, a cyclone of hues, and the current sweeps him up and under. He is six and the world is before him, no past, only present, the future impossible to see or hold, as the tide swallows the shore. He holds his breath, waits for the scene to clear, but the night is silence and shadows and the future is stuffed in his lab coat pocket, locked away, impossible to reach. Nonna is dead and buried. He is alone.

Stumbling on the sidewalk, he peers ahead, searching in the dark for his own front steps. He pushes his fingers into his eyes. How tired he is, how far he's come. He shuffles on, the thin soles scraping pavement. Now he thinks only of the soft cheeks of his son, the sweet perfume of his daughter, the warm hand of his wife. One foot after the other he walks on, the corner, the neighbor's, the gray slate of his own stoop. His feet ache, but the light at his door burns as strongly as the Mediterranean sun.

Manners and Morals

Deborah M. Prum

(This is a chapter excerpted from the novel-in-progress *Smiling on the Inside*)

October 1962

Sammy's mother had bad eyes. On Saturday nights, sometimes Mrs. D'Angelo would pay Sammy and me a nickel a piece to spot numbers on her bingo cards at the game at Our Lady church. Ma was happy to let me go. It gave her time to play cards with Aunt Connie and Uncle Carl at the VFW.

One evening as we walked into the church, the new priest, Father Menditto, cornered Mrs. D'Angelo. "Rita, could you step into my office? I'd like to speak with you about your boy, Julian." Father Menditto rubbed his shiny chin with his fingertips. Father had no hair on his face, just really light eyebrows.

"You wanna talk about my Julian? We can talk right here." Mrs. D'Angelo didn't like missing any part of the bingo game and she didn't like anyone saying bad stuff about her oldest son. She idolized fifteen-year-old Julian. But she didn't think so highly of her youngest. Everybody in the neighborhood knew that she had wanted a girl when Sammy was born.

Father Menditto looked at Sammy and me. I could tell he wished he didn't have to discuss anything in front of us.

"Rita, I think maybe your son has a little problem. Every time he serves as an altar boy, we seem to be missing a statue or a cup afterward." Father sniffed and brushed invisible lint from his black pants.

"Yeah. So?" Mrs. D'Angelo poked through her purse, looking for money to buy the bingo cards.

Father Menditto bent down toward Mrs. D'Angelo, trying to get her attention. "We think he might be taking them."

"My Juli? He would never do nothing like that. You find yourself another thief." Mrs. D'Angelo pushed past the priest and marched down stairs to the church basement to start her games.

Of course, I didn't say a word. But Julian stealing statues sounded about right to me. More than once, I'd seen him come out of the corner grocery store with his pockets stuffed with candy or cigarettes or whatever he could lay his hands on.

After helping Mrs. D'Angelo through several rounds of bingo, Sammy and I stood behind the refreshment table. Mrs. D'Angelo allowed us to have one piece of pastry each. However, we discovered if we kept smiling at everyone who passed by, we could sneak as many as four or five cookies off the trays.

After we stuffed our pockets, we slipped out to the church kitchen. Sammy bit into a cookie and then wiped the sugar from his lips. "I don't give two hoots about those statues. Really, Julian could burn them up for all I care. But, I sure would like to get him in trouble."

I fished a candy-covered almond out of my pocket and popped it into my mouth. "Do you think Julian swiped that junk?"

"Dunno. But I bet if he did, he'd hide them in the garage." Sammy grinned as he ate the last of the cookie.

So, the next afternoon Sammy and I began searching the D'Angelos' garage. After a few minutes, Sammy found some bags under his father's workbench.

"BINGO! Look at this stuff, Tina." Sammy ripped open a paper sack. Julian had broken the statues to pieces. Heads, arms, legs tumbled out.

Sammy and I threw the stolen goods back into the bag and ran up to the D'Angelos' apartment. His mother sat at the kitchen table sipping black coffee and listening to Mario Lanza full blast on her record player.

"Hey Ma, look what I found in the garage." Sammy dumped the holy object body parts on the table.

Mrs. D'Angelo's eyes bugged out and she sat straight up. "JULI! Get out here right now!"

Julian came into the kitchen, yawned and stretched. His T-shirt lifted to show his hairy belly. "Ya woke me up, Ma."

"You better wake up. Where did these things come from?" Mrs. D'Angelo pointed to what looked like the remains of a massacre on her kitchen table.

Julian blinked and then stared down at his black high-top sneakers. He was the only person I knew who slept with his sneakers on. "Ain't never seen them before."

Mrs. D'Angelo dragged Julian down to the parish house to return the statue pieces. Sammy and I tagged along, hoping to see some fireworks.

After Father Menditto took a look inside the bag, he put his hand on Mrs. D'Angelo's shoulder. "I know you don't have a lot of money right now. I'll think of some odd jobs Julian can do to work off the cost of replacing what he broke."

Mrs. D'Angelo didn't say a word.

Father studied his nails for a moment. "Maybe we should think about having him talk with me or one of the other priests. Just to help him with whatever is going on."

"I didn't do nothing. Honest, Ma." Julian looked her straight in the eye.

Mrs. D'Angelo turned toward the door. "I gotta believe my boy. You're not gonna see us in this church anymore." She walked out of Our Lady that day and never went back. Not even for bingo.

The very next week, as soon as Julian could figure out how to hot wire a car, he stole two. The second one happened to belong to a retired probation officer. Soon after, a judge sent Julian to Bellshire Reformatory.

Anyway, that's how Sammy wound up with me in Manners and Morals class. On Wednesday afternoons at two o'clock, most children at Howley elementary went off to some sort of religious training: catechism, Hebrew school, Lutheran Youth. Nonreligious kids and kids whose families were on the outs with the church (like my mother and Sammy's mother) attended Manners and Morals class at Howley.

For an hour-and-a-half each Wednesday, the staff at the school took turns teaching the class to the thirty children who were left behind. Most of teachers thought of the ninety minutes as a long recess. They showed us slides of their vacations and let us play hangman on the blackboard.

The one exception was Miss O'Keefe, a teacher who had been in the business at least forty years. She took our manners and morals training seriously.

On one gray Wednesday afternoon, Miss O'Keefe sat on a chair in front of our class with a grim look on her face. Her short chubby legs swung back and forth above the floor as she spoke.

"Class, I have a terrrrible story to tell you." She emphasized each of her words by pointing her thumb at us, her dead father's gold ring shoved down on the knuckle.

Miss O'Keefe raised her bushy eyebrows. "Once there was a boy named Georgie. Yes. Georgie Costello. Yes." Miss O'Keefe yanked on one curl of her dyed red hair and twisted it around her finger. Ma and Aunt Angie always joked about Miss O'Keefe's hair. They said she permed it into a frenzy.

"Georgie lived with his grandparents in an old house. He was a rude, nasty child, the kind who grabbed the last cookie on the plate, then talked with his mouth full." Miss O'Keefe's nostrils flared and she looked as if she might spit.

"Georgie's grandma always warned him, 'Don't you go in the cellar, George Costello. There's bad things down there.'" Miss O'Keefe's stump legs were really pumping now.

"So one day, rude nasty George stole three jelly-filled powdered doughnuts." She leaned forward. "The last ones in the box. And, he sneaked off to the basement to eat them."

"Georgie got down in that cellar. He didn't put a light on. Noooooo. He didn't want to get caught."

Miss O'Keefe lowered her voice so we all had to bend forward to hear. "What do you think happened?"

Poor Dickie Chambers, a kid with a huge head, started rocking in his seat and moaning, "Oh no . . . oh no . . . oh no. . . ." Another boy bopped him with a book to make him stop.

Miss O'Keefe jumped up and started shouting: "A big hairy man sprung out at him. Dressed all in green. Escaped from the county pen. He had long, gray fingernails and only one ear."

Then Miss O'Keefe sat back in her chair and smoothed down her black skirt. Rumor was that she always dressed in black out of respect for her father who'd died years ago. She just stared out of the window for a few seconds.

That was too much for Sammy. "Golly, Miss O'Keefe, what the heck happened?"

Miss O'Keefe neatly folded her hands in her lap. "We don't know, dear. All they found was doughnut crumbs and powdered sugar on the basement floor." Then, for the first time that hour, Miss O'Keefe smiled at us.

When the bell rang, I felt a thrill of pure relief as we bolted from the classroom. We ran to our clubhouse, a moldy brick-walled alley between covered by a tarpaper roof. I arrived first and pushed through the burlap door. I screamed when I saw a figure crouched by the back wall.

"Shut up, Tina, just shut up." Julian whispered as he jumped toward me.

I ducked away from him. "Don't touch me. I'll be quiet."

Sammy scooted back, too. "Why aren't you at Bellshire, Julian? I'm telling Ma."

Julian yanked Sammy all the way into the alley and slammed him against the wall. "You open your mouth and I'll bust your head in half." Then, Julian covered his face with his hands and sobbed.

"Okay. We won't tell." I had never seen Julian cry before. I felt like throwing up.

"The guys at Bellshire, they thought I ratted on them to the guards. They beat the living daylights outta me." Julian looked up. His cheek was bruised and he had a long cut on his neck. "I can't go back there." Julian rubbed his cheek.

"What are you going to do?" I knew Julian couldn't hide out in the alley for very long.

"I need bus money. If I can get to Vermont, I can work at the apple orchards up there. A guy at Bellshire told me all about it."

"How much you need?" Sammy surprised me by acting interested in what happened to Julian.

"Bus fare to Bellows Falls is about five bucks. I can catch the bus at Jimmy's Smoke Shop downtown." Julian stood up and began to pace.

"Where are we going to get the money?" Sammy looked worried.

I knew I couldn't help. Recently, I'd swiped my picture out of Ma's wallet. Since then, she kept her purse hidden in the apartment.

"Sammy, you know Ma's got at least five dollars stashed in her bingo jar. Maybe you can get hold of that."

Sammy and I looked at each other. Miss O'Keefe's story was still fresh in our minds. Sammy spoke first. "Okay, Julian. We'll get the jar."

You could count on Sammy's mother to react to blood. So, we decided to scrape Sammy's knee on the concrete steps by his house.

Once we had him bleeding hard, we charged into their apartment. I screamed, "He's hurt. He's hurt." Sammy yowled and held his bleeding knee.

While Mrs. D'Angelo patched up Sammy in the bathroom, I rushed into her bedroom and grabbed the jar from her dresser. The jar sat in front of a living color picture of the Virgin Mary praying. A halo glowed around her head. She seemed to be staring straight at me. I paused, but only for a second. Then, as Sammy created a ruckus in the bathroom, I bounded down the stairs with the jar under my jacket. The loose change clinked when my foot hit each step.

I dashed through the backyard and into the alley. "Here's the cash, Julian."

"Thanks, Tina. I owe ya." Julian dumped the money onto the concrete and began counting it.

"Don't mention it to anyone. Not to anyone. Ever."

So, as I headed off to supper at Nonnie's, I tried to figure out if I was a hero or a criminal. Julian was no saint. In fact, we'd all be safer if he was in reform school. But if the cops sent him back to Bellshire, for sure, he'd get beaten up or worse.

I knew I shouldn't steal, especially not with the Blessed Mother watching me. Yet, she looked so kind and merciful. I'll bet she would have slipped him the bingo money, too.

Next to the Fortune-Teller's House

Jody Hobbs Hesler

We lived here six months before the sign went up—the neon-lighted palm, as tall as me standing. Before the sign, we didn't know what all those people wanted with her, our gray-haired neighbor with the gypsy clothes. Now a line of people wait for the neon hand to click on mornings. Used to be, they just lined up with the light of day.

It's too early now for the lines. I wake slowly, to a distant, smoky scent. I hobble, half-blind, to the window that looks out toward the fortune-teller's property. In a dark spot fifty yards or so downhill from her house, a hundred yards from mine, a smudge of light smolders.

Our houses front the back road to the airport. Our yards are long and wide. Beyond us on one side, for sale signs pepper undeveloped woods and predict strip malls and office parks. On the other side, just beyond the fortune-teller's house, stands a gas station. We're all either of us has for neighbors.

A few times before the sign, I made a pot of tea, laid some ginger cookies on a plate, and arranged it all on a tray. Once, I made it halfway across my yard before the cars started pulling up in the fortune-teller's driveway. I stood with my tray and stared. I'd seen them before, but the steady streams are always a surprise. Sometimes there are priests, sometimes cops. What does she tell them?

She can't be awake over there now. No light shines out from the house, though the front yard flames grow brighter as I watch. My husband grunts from the sheets, half asleep, "Evelyn? Are you coming back to bed?"

If I'd made it over to the fortune-teller's house that first time with the cookies and the tea, I would have asked her, What will my baby be when she grows up? Will she look more like my husband or me? Will she be happy? But shortly after my first effort at visiting, that baby died inside me.

The next time I was ready to arrange cookies and tea on a tray, I would've asked simpler things—Will this baby have all its toes? Curly hair or straight?

After the second one died, I was afraid to meet the fortune-teller at all, afraid to learn if I'd get pregnant again or if another baby might die. Even if I chose not to ask her anything, I was afraid of what I'd see in her eyes when we met. I started to dislike her.

I move to the front of the house to another window that looks out onto the fortune-teller's yard. The little fire wavers into the darkness. Is it part of a ritual? I think it isn't. But I don't know what sorts of things fortune-tellers might go in for.

I do know she's a gardener, though. On the rare moments when there are no lines of people waiting for her, she crouches in her yard, tending her plants. Butterflies light on her hair. Her garden is perfect with blossoms. She positions cement benches in thoughtful spaces around her yard. Sometimes, the people waiting for her sit there, seeming to be calmed by the living things around them.

For every baby who dies, I plant a lilac or rose of Sharon in our yard. I'll see the blossoms every spring of every year we live here and remember the babies whose lives slipped away before I could even touch their warm, petal-smooth skin. I'm afraid I'll have a fat healthy hedge as an old, old lady, and no children, no grandchildren. Just beautiful shrubs and tiny, fey ghosts swirling through the greenery.

The smoke thickens across the way. Are the smoke-clouds meant to carry some kind of message?

At the fortune-teller's house lately, a man comes whenever the sign is off. I've seen him from across our yard. He's burly with a rough-sounding voice that I can hear sometimes, when the air is right. I've heard him shout at her once or twice. I'm not the fortune-teller, but there's something wrong about that man.

It's been a long time since I last thought of going next door to meet my neighbor, a long time since I became afraid of her. Now is my third pregnancy.

What would the fortune-teller have seen if I'd managed to visit while pregnant with one of the babies who died? Would the tea leaves have arranged themselves in the bases of our cups in death-shaped prophesies? If so, or if she could have known some other way, would she have told me? Would she have had a choice?

I wake up each morning thinking of polar bears. When it isn't cold enough for them anymore, they'll all die. One day, there will be a last polar bear. Is today my baby's last day? Is my body her shrinking ice cap?

If you say something like that with a doctor listening, something mystical and worried, they prescribe pregnancy-friendly antidepressants or refer you to a support group. I don't want these things. I just want my babies.

The fire eats away at what appears to be a shrub in one of the many landscaped areas of the fortune-teller's yard, near one of her benches. I can picture that man who visits her, sneaking from their bed under the cover of darkness, pouring gasoline on her favorite bush, tossing a match.

Did she know at the first soft look in that man's eye that he would turn into a devil and bring destruction? And then did she choose to love him anyway, as long as his gentleness lasted?

My nightgown trails the high, late-spring meadow grass that separates our houses. I'm running. The burning bush crackles in my ears. I run past the bonfire heat of it, then cut toward the house, short of breath, my feet scratching against dry grass and tiny rocks.

At the fortune-teller's door, I drape one hand across my belly. Maybe my lost babies have known the feeling of my arm's cradle, at least.

I pound the fortune-teller's door in the shadow of the tall palm-shaped sign, now dark. Dawn has made the sky white. A few cars curl away on the road in front of our houses. The day's first plane has not yet taken off.

What will I do if that burly man is still here, if he answers the door?

But he won't. Somehow I know the fire's all he's left behind.

I've never seen the fortune-teller up close. Her face pinches with wrinkles, like a wizened fruit left on a window sill. She looks weary. She doesn't stand straight, leans into the door when she opens it. My hand reaches out to hers. "I saw the fire. Are you all right?"

"Fire?" she says, not alarmed exactly. She wasn't awake before my knock. She casts a glance over my shoulder, sees the flames from the bush licking the sky above it. She nods. "Fire." A look of resignation takes over the features of her face. She opens the door wider for me.

I step inside. "I'm so sorry."

She nods again and leads me to her kitchen. Her white nightgown is thin as paper, and her feet are bare. Her hands dangle, empty, at her sides. Like a little child. I think how everyone is a little child.

"Let's have some tea," she says. And she can tell I've figured out something very sad and secret about her life. This is a morning like dozens of other mornings she's had. She'll have other mornings like it. I'm sorry to know this.

When she pours the tea, she sits across from me at her breakfast table. Her feet don't touch the ground. "I'm Evelyn," I say. "I've meant to come meet you, ever since we moved in."

"I know," she says, but she doesn't mean it in a fortune-telling way. "It isn't easy to visit me with all the people coming and going. I've meant to come meet you, too, but then the next one comes." She waves her hand toward the front door. I picture fortunes, like liquid, draining from her over the years. She must be very tired.

"Should we put out the fire?" I say.

"No, it'll be all right, Evelyn."

I don't know if this is a fortune or not. I don't know if she means the fire will put itself out; if she means the man will not come back; if she means this baby will live. But it doesn't matter. This is just a cup of tea with the fortune-teller next door, who is soon to be my friend. It will be all right.

Dreamtime

Phyllis Anne Duncan

(Winner of the 2014 Second Annual Flash Fiction Online
Flash-versary contest)

In dreams on walkabout, my ancestors in the rock paintings come alive and descend to my camp. They circle my puny fire and dance, shadows against the star-filled night. They speak to me in the ancient tongue, and my soul understands if my brain doesn't.

A dancer hands me his didgeridoo, and I press my lips to the mouthpiece, shaped by countless others, taste the beeswax, feel it soften and mold to my mouth. I breathe, the buzz-hum surrounds me, swirls into the night, and the unbroken arm of the Milky Way vibrates as it did when the first player breathed music into a virgin atmosphere.

Am I the first to lift the didgeridoo toward the stars, place the mouthpiece before my eye, and peer down the termite-hewn length to see the universe shrunken to a bright ball of light?

I think of the days spent seeking the right dead tree, the hours of fingers thumping along its length to test the hollowness, the weeks of hands smoothing the outside, of preparing the paints, of the first to exhale into it, which gave it life. No two are alike. Passed from father to son, only the sons until the mothers and sisters and daughters insisted they share the music. They made it richer.

In daylight at work, I aim the radio telescope where I have looked with my didgeridoo and listen for a signal. The hiss-crack of static has a familiar sound, as if some alien with thinned aboriginal blood has sent its song into space toward this speck in the sky. We are kindred spirits, that alien dream-walker and I, for am I not the alien here, my face the only dark one among the pale?

"Where do you go on the weekends?" they ask, but I don't tell them. They would never understand walkabout or dreamtime, never understand how I feel more welcome among the spirits. I cannot render spirits into binary code or strings of numbers denoting cosmic distances, which the others would comprehend. If I tried to explain dancing with my ancestors, they would exchange looks, laugh behind my back at the "crazy abo."

They will never be painted onto the rocks.

When it is my time—when the spirits tell me—I will go walkabout and not return, like my father and grandfathers all the way back to the ones painted on the rocks. I will play the didgeridoo one final time, sending its music skyward for some distant radio astronomer to chalk up as an anomaly. But another dream-walker will hear and understand and mourn my passing. The earth will take me within its womb again, and I will hear countless didgeridoos playing my dirge. When our sun dies and blasts my atoms into the void, I will carry the song to the far ends of the universe where other suns will form and my atoms will make a new dream-walker to be painted on the rocks.

Then, in dreams on walkabout, I will descend and dance around a fire.

Blood and Guts

Phyllis Anne Duncan

(First place fiction, Blue Ridge Writers VWC, 2015)

He woke to the smell most familiar to him in all the world—freshly turned earth, rich, loamy, a smell he never tired of, even after hours of plowing.

He bolted upright. If he'd fallen asleep while taking a break, his brother Eddie would—

The man blinked and looked around. Soldiers as far as he could see. They lounged about, smoking, playing cards. Tanks moved back and forth, churning up dirt. Well, nothing had changed. His unit was still stuck on this side of the river, the engineers' pontoon bridge still spanned that river, and tanks still tried to cross it.

"Morning, Sarge," came from behind him.

For a moment, he wanted to look around for Sergeant Warren; then, he remembered. A German soldier's lucky shot had sent Warren home in a box and made Gabriel Day a sergeant two days after his eighteenth birthday. The L.T. had said that made him one of the youngest, if not the youngest, in the Army.

"Morning, Goose," Day said. "They still at it?"

"Yeah. Lots of guys are grumbling, especially a few tanks before it's their turn to try to cross."

Sergeant Day shook his head. He'd learned pretty quick the officers were just as new to war as he was.

Day had never been much beyond the boundaries of the Commonwealth of Virginia until basic training had brought him to Fort Dix, New Jersey. From there he had crossed the Atlantic, going in the opposite direction from his ancestors, who'd fled when Bonnie Prince Charlie lost at Culloden. He'd come ashore in France in his tank just days after D-day and had fought across fields so lush he could almost think he was back in Culpeper County.

Yeah, not bad for a farmer from Virginia in the Third Army, Fourth Armored Division, 25th Mechanized Cavalry Recon, and kicking German ass on the way to Berlin.

Except, well, they'd been held up here for days now, trying to cross a river. More like a wide stream really, but the opposite bank had a short bluff, just big enough to hide one of those German Tiger tanks. The Germans had let them build the pontoon bridge, but when the first tank had gotten halfway across, that German tank had popped up over the ridge and put a shell into the Sherman. Then it had disappeared before the American tanks could swing their turrets and open fire.

It had taken time to clear the hulk of the burning tank from the bridge, recover the bodies or pieces of the men, and start the stupid dance all over again.

Why the hell don't the L.T. just go to another part of the river, he'd wondered. Maybe the Germans didn't blow up all the bridges, but he knew they had. It's what he would have done, just like his hero from the War Between the States, John S. Mosby.

So far, they'd lost six tanks.

"Why don't the L.T. send some guys across the river?" Day asked Goose.

"He's had volunteers. He figures he needs permission or some such," Goose said. "I heard talk last night, if we don't get across that river soon, old Blood and Guts himself is showing up."

Not the first time Gen. George Patton had arrived to urge them onward. Most of the guys hated the old man, but Patton was a Virginia Military Institute graduate, just like the eldest son in every generation of Day's family, and that was all Day needed to follow him.

"Maybe that'll put some lead in the L.T.'s pencil," Day said. "I need to check something out, Goose. Catch up with you later."

Day headed off into the woods, looking for the right tree, and he found an old red oak with branches dipping low. He climbed, going up until the branches could barely hold his weight. He brought out his binoculars and scanned the countryside. The river took a sharp bend about two hundred yards to the south of the pontoon bridge, and he could see it was a little wider there. He noted the change in the color of the water. It was shallower there, too, but he could see why the engineers rejected it as a crossing point—a wall of solid rock perpendicular to the ground on the opposite shore. The Sherman could cross some incredibly steep terrain, but it sure couldn't go vertical.

Day stayed high up in the oak, studying, planning. When the German tank emerged to blow up the next hapless Sherman on the bridge, he got a good look at it. How many men in the crew? Five, he recalled from his training.

But what made him think it was just this one tank?

Well, if there were more than one, why didn't they all start firing on the sitting-duck Americans across the way?

No, this was a straggler or maybe a crew ordered to stay behind and keep us from crossing the river.

He climbed down from the tree and went to his tank. From his duffel he took a carton of cigarettes his mother had sent. He concealed that inside his jacket and strolled over to one of the infantry units. After a few minutes of dickering, he had what he wanted and handed the cigarettes over in payment. He went back to his tank and waited for dark.

* * * *

Holding the M9 bazooka as high over his head as his arms would stretch, Gabriel Day waded across the stream at the shallow spot he'd scouted from the tree that morning. He took it slow because he didn't want to step into a hole or a drop-off, which would end this fool's errand pretty damn quick.

He wasn't even sure why he was doing this. He wanted to finish his part in this war, get home, and do the only thing he'd ever desired—settle on his section of the farm, where he could build his own house, work his land, and have a life, which might someday include a wife and children who would love farming as much as he did. He could keep his head down, not take chances, and he'd be back on the farm his family had worked since 1749.

Instead, he was up to his armpits in chilly water, going after an enemy tank on an unauthorized mission. He was tired of sitting around waiting to be the one to try and cross that fucking pontoon bridge, tired of lieutenants who couldn't or wouldn't command, and if this cost him the stripe he'd just earned, so be it. What it couldn't cost was his life. Like Blood and Guts Patton once said, "You win wars by making the other poor bastards die for their country."

Some Germans were going to die for their Fatherland tonight, then.

He thought he made far too much noise scrambling up the embankment, but no bullets came his way. Staying low to the ground, he crept forward until the silhouette of the Tiger stood out in the starlight. Damn, but it looked fucking huge. What the hell did he think he was doing? He'd come this far, though, so he slipped from tree to tree until he felt he was within thirty yards of the tank. Because of the tank's armor, that was the limit of the M9's effectiveness, but he wanted to make this a sure thing. He edged forward until fewer than twenty yards lay between him and the Tiger.

His studied the tank, located the spot he wanted, and knelt, settling the bazooka on his shoulder.

The explosion made his ears ring, but he dropped the bazooka and brought up his .45. The Tiger's hatch popped open, and men began to launch themselves from the burning tank. The first two were like some horror movie, on fire and screaming. He shot them mainly to keep them quiet. A third man fell from the hatch to the ground and groaned. He wasn't on fire, but he lay there and whimpered. Day's eyes went from him to the tank hatch. There should be two more. The minutes passed, the flames making the clearing bright as daytime. No more men came from the tank. They were fried inside. Good. They'd done that to too many of his buddies.

The one survivor had rolled over onto his belly to drag himself toward Day. Day strode forward, arm extended, finger on the trigger of the .45. The German turned his soot-stained face up and raised an empty hand toward Day.

"*Kamerad!*" he said. "*Kamerad! Bitte nicht schiessen!*"

Like most of his buddies, Day had learned a few German phrases. He recognized the word for friend and *nicht schiessen*. The low-life German coward didn't want to be shot. Too fucking bad. Day's buddies in the Shermans hadn't wanted to die either.

The German got to his knees and raised his hands. "*Amerikaner*," he said, "I surrender."

The English startled Day for a moment, but he kept coming until he could have reached out and put the muzzle of the .45 on the man's forehead. He never thought he could look someone in the eye and shoot them, but right now, he knew he could.

The fire in the tank flared and showed Day the German's face in absolute clarity. Bright, blue eyes in a face no older than fourteen or fifteen pleaded with him.

An enemy had reached the point of desperation when it had old men and children fighting its wars, and this boy was the same age as Day's younger brother.

He lowered his arm. "*Sprechen Englisch?*" he asked.

"*Ja.* Some. *Bitte*, I want go home. *Meinen Bruder*, all killed. *Mein Vater* has no one to work *bauerhof*," the Kraut said.

"What's a *bauerhof?*"

"Where we grow food."

The Germans were the enemy, he knew. Monsters. Evil incarnate. They weren't supposed to be people you could relate to. "You farm?" Day asked.

"*Ja, ja.* If I die, *mein Vater* has no one for farm."

Day raised the gun again. "You better not be lying to me. *Nicht lüge.*"

"I swear, I swear! On my mother!"

Damn, Day thought. He lowered the gun once more, his thoughts racing. Here they were, two farmers doing a job neither of them was suited to.

"All right," Day said, decision made, "go on, but no more killing Americans. *Amerikaners, nicht*, uh, *tötung.*"

"I promise. No more killing Americans."

Day waved with the gun. "Go on before I change my mind."

"*Danke*," the boy said and scrambled to his feet. He ran a few yards away, then turned. Day kept the .45 at the ready. "What is your name?" the boy asked.

"I'm Sgt. Gabriel Day, U.S. Army. I'm a farmer, too."

The boy smiled. "I am Oskar Hueber. Some day I come to America. We have beer, *ja*, and talk farming?"

46

"Yeah, sure."

Day watched until Oskar disappeared into the forest; then, he picked up the M9 and headed back the way he came.

* * * *

"Day," said the L.T., "I don't know whether to court-martial you or put you in for a medal."

"The medal's not necessary, sir," Day said. "I just did what had to be done, but if you think I should be court-martialed, well, nothing I can say will change that."

The L.T. tried to look stern, but he was all of maybe twenty-three and worked in a grocery store back in the States. He didn't pull it off at all.

"Damn, Day, you took out a tank and killed its entire crew on your own. You saved lives and got us back on schedule. How the hell could I court-martial you for that? Get outta here and get your tank ready to move, but, Sergeant, don't you ever do anything like that again. Unless you tell me first."

Day drew himself up to attention, saluted, then about-faced. He left the lieutenant's tent, content he'd saved his buddies, even if they might die later. Today they lived, as did one German boy, Day's secret to keep.

Tanks rolled by, and he breathed in the scent of freshly turned earth, the smell most familiar to him in all the world.

Petite Small

Elaine Ruggieri

(Honorable mention, Virginia Writers Club Summer Shorts, 2014)

The average woman's height in the United States is 5 feet. 3.8 inches. I miss by 4 inches. Dr. Ruth is 4 feet. 7 inches; Madeleine Albright, 4 feet, 10 inches; and *Jersey Shore*'s Nicole "Snooki" Polizzi, 4 feet, 9 inches. We short women cannot be judged by vertical dimensions alone.

I was always the "runt of the litter." Strangers would ask if I had started school yet. I was in the third grade!

My taller high school girlfriends thought I was "so cute," as if I were their playmate, The Talking Doll. "Lucky you. You can date anyone," they'd say.

I didn't date.

After high school and college I realized how much I preferred small things: compact cars, little cans of peas, mini-Milky Ways, dot-sized earrings, scant portions of pasta, anything slight, petite, tiny, modest, measured, and simple—nothing looming large, elaborate, loud, or lunch in a restaurant with more than four people. I never bought a gigantic box of Tide, and certainly not an SUV. I drive a Beetle and stock travel-size toothpastes. But, I always liked tall men, maybe something to do with a future gene pool.

Today I am shopping for a new dress to wear to a big party. Petite sizes are somewhat new to the ladies' fashion world. There were none available when I finally grew out of the children's department. My only choice was Misses Small, which had to be raised at the shoulders and shortened at the hem. Now there are whole departments dedicated to diminutive women. Unfortunately, the petite merchandise often mirrors the regular sizes "sewn small" as in Petite 4 or Petite 6, or are labeled in redundant sizes like PP (Petite Petite) and PS (Petite Small)—with little consideration to styling for the short.

A saleswoman approaches, slender and towering. She has the ideal figure for the pencil skirt. She looks down and says, "May I help you with a *little* something?" I resent the *size* reference.

"I'm looking for a dress. Not too dressy and not too casual, but I haven't seen anything I like in my size.?"

"Which is??" she asks, looking at me from top to bottom. I straighten up and inhale deeply.

"Petite Small or Petite 6, maybe P4," I answer and add quickly, "Sizes lie."

"Sometimes," she says. "Let's see." She leads me with a runway swagger to a rack of dresses in splashy prints of pink, lemon, and aquamarine, a pale one's palette, perfect for the "summer/spring" complexion types. But, not for me, a brunette, and most definitely a "winter," according to a supermarket magazine.

"Not my colors," I say. "And, I can't wear those large, crazy prints. I'm too short."

"Try them anyway. They can go anywhere, perfect for the cruise season," she says as she swings a tangerine number from the rack and holds it up against herself. She is at least 5 feet, 11 inches, blonde, and long, long-legged. She could have worn a wine-stained tablecloth and still looked chic.

I shake my head. "No Love Boats in my future. Don't think so." I try to sound decisive, but her tallness and chic-ness intimidate me. I look away thinking, "Thank God, I don't have to try on bathing suits!"

"Ooookay. Let's move on. Do you like knits?" the elegant stork asks, with obvious disdain for such practical fabrics.

"If they don't cling around my bottom, yes."

"Look through these then. And, if you need me, I'll be over there," she says and points to the busy Misses section. Striding away in her stiletto heels and lime-green pants, she hurries to help a 5-feet, 7-inch, Misses 10. Uppity blonde! May she sit in Economy Class for a ten-hour flight!

I hang two knit dresses, dark brown in sizes Petite 4 and Petite 6 in the dressing room and begin the dreaded trying-on dance. The mirror provides three different ways to see that the P4 bunches in rolls around my butt and can go no farther without tugs and pulls. Why didn't I wear pantyhose? Lycra, I need!

Next I try the P6, but the brown looks like mud. Although it slides down more easily, the fabric curves around my seat in a perfect question mark, asking "Tight enough?"

Dressing rooms are airless, claustrophobic cells. I begin to perspire, and the lingering smell of citrus perfume and shopworn clothing makes me sneeze. Am I really that lumpy *there?* I ask myself in the fun-house mirror. The fluorescent lights hum while my skin turns sallow.

I wonder where Stork Legs is and if she'll come to see how I'm doing. Impatient and dejected, I throw on my own clothes and go for another search for dresses in P6 or P Small. Ah, there's her High-ness in the Misses section cashing out a customer.

She holds up a finger and then sashays in my direction. "Have you tried anything yet?"

"Just those knits! They fit like a sock with the heel in the back."

"Knits can do that," she says. Yeah, but not on her body, I think.

"Sorry I couldn't help you. Got busy. Look, give those dresses over there a chance. You might be surprised."

At the rack she first showed me, I snatch up an armful of P6s and P Smalls, all in shades of tropical fruits, and hurry back to the dressing room.

I spot a Petite Small in a deep, pinkish shade, like the dark flesh of a ripe watermelon. I hold it against myself, and think, *This short winter person can wear this.* I twist the price tag around. $68. Can even afford it. Better yet, wear it to the party. It fits!

I am triumphant as I leave the stifling room with the dress over my arm. "I see you found something," says my sylphlike saleswoman as she approaches.

"Yes, I was lucky," I say. "I need it for tonight."

"If you have a store card, you get 20 percent off today. Lucky twice," she says, looking at the dress. "This is a great color for you."

I know she's waiting for me to acknowledge she was right all along, but I don't. She carefully hangs the dress in a garment bag, knots the bottom, and holds it even with her shoulders. I have to stretch to reach it like a game of keep-away. "Thanks for your help," I finally say and hand her my charge card.

"It's perfect for your petite figure," she says. At least she didn't tell me good things come in small packages. "So, big bash tonight?"

"Anniversary party. You know—lots of single women and few eligible men. But, they'll all be trimmed out."

"You'll look great. Sorry I didn't see it on you."

"I dressed fast. Afraid I'd change my mind."

She laughs, and says, "I do that too. Your signature, please"

"But you can wear anything," I murmur as I look down and sign.

"Not always." She looks me over. "Three-inch heels are what you need. Follow me. The shoe department's having a big sale."

Regretting my small-mindedness about her tallness, I follow her eagerly, confident she'll find me a pair of spike heels to raise me up.

Selective Memory

Elaine Ruggieri

(Second place fiction, Blue Ridge Writers Chapter VWC, 2015)

Gina's knees touch her mother's as she sits in front of her, holding her freckled hands. Her mother quickly rearranges herself on the La-Z-Boy recliner. Then she hits the lift button and settles her legs on the footrest. Gina has to move away quickly.

"Give me some warning next time, will ya?" says Gina. She just misses being kneecapped.

"Sorry, I had a sudden cramp. This footrest springs up pretty fast, I know, but it's good for my legs."

Gina knows better. Her mother, Bev, never liked "touchy feely" stuff, like holding hands, and now that she's in a senior living facility, dislikes it more. "They want to hug me or pat my head all the time. I'm not some lapdog," she often complains.

"Will you be all right, then?" Gina asks. "I'll be gone just for four days. Squaw Valley, remember? Skiing. You have my cell number, right?"

"Right in my phone. Of course, I'll be all right. Isn't that why you gave me this so-called panic necklace and this iridescent cane? One strangles me and the other makes me trip, plus the damn thing shines in the dark and keeps me awake. Look how bright it is." Bev holds the cane up to the sunlight. "See!" she says and lets it drop to the floor.

Gina pushes it closer to her with her foot. "It's so you can find it at night, Mother. Other residents have them in case of an emergency."

"Then I'd be a goner," says Bev. "You read the papers. They never get patients in these places out in time. Them first, not us." She shakes her head in disapproval. "And, for God's sake, stop calling us residents. It implies we reside here."

"And, you don't?" Gina asks, smiling at her mother's crossness.

"Not willingly or permanently. Residents. Phuh! We're like prisoners serving out a life term, confined by age and infirmities. And convenience for our families, of course." She gives Gina a telling look.

It's a familiar accusation and Gina ignores it now. She felt guilty when she first agreed with Dr. Haynes that Bev needed some assisted care but has come to realize it was wise advice. With all her complaints, Bev's health, mobility, and even her memory have improved at Healthy Horizons. Everything but her attitude. Would I be any different, Gina often asks herself?

One of the "unwilling residents" looks in at the door, and Gina welcomes the interruption. Today is not the day to feel more regret, deserved or not. "Oh, hi, Mrs. Drumley. Doing okay?"

"It's Gina, isn't it?"

Gina nods.

"Good as can be expected, dearie," Mrs. Drumley says with a sigh. "The arthritis comes and goes. Some days worse than others. Remember, Bev. Lunch in twenty minutes. Bring Gina," she says at the open doorway and then pushes her walker forward.

"Damn busybody!" says Bev.

"Shh. She'll hear you, Mother."

"Shut the door. I've already told Miss Nosey to mind her own business, and stop reminding me about meals. Lunch soon, Bev." She imitates Mrs. Drumley. "She's always the first one in the dining room and wants me to keep her company."

"Well, she's just trying to be nice and neighborly," says Gina while straightening Bev's collar. "This blouse never did stay down around your neck. It curls up."

Bev shakes her shoulders and pushes Gina's hands away. "Nice gets you nothing here. The few bony men die fast and the women are bossy. They tell lies too, especially about their grandchildren. All perfect citizens."

"Oh, so you don't brag a little about our Joey?" asks Gina, still looking at Bev's stubborn collar.

"Only if they ask and I make it simple. They don't understand high tech and I can't explain it. I just say he's going to be a multimillionaire before he's thirty. They don't believe it anyway. And, God knows, they won't remember it."

"I can stay for lunch with you, if you'd like. It's pizza day, isn't it? It was pretty good the last time," says Gina.

"Hard to ruin pizza, but they try. Sure, stay, but only if we can get a table for two. I don't want company. Especially Mrs. Drumley."

"You like Pete. Maybe he'll join us," says Gina. She's dreading a one-on-one lunch with her mother in the dining room. Because of the long silences, she always eats too fast and then she has indigestion for the rest of the afternoon. Her mother eats little and complains about the food and Mrs. Drumley.

Sometimes Gina brings lunch so they can eat together in Bev's apartment, away from all the residents Bev wants to avoid. When they do, Bev's attention centers on the unfamiliar deli food, so she doesn't ask so many personal questions. The kind Gina wants to dodge.

"Doubt if old Pete will be there. Pizza gives his stomach fits, and his days are numbered, poor guy," says Bev with some surprising sympathy in her voice.

"There are other things he can eat. Soup, sandwiches," says Gina.

"Oh, let's forget lunch, Gina. I can eat later. Don't you have lots to do before you leave?" Bev asks and wipes her nose with a plaid handkerchief she uses only when she has visitors. Although Gina brings her lots of tissues, Bev uses them sparingly. Instead she keeps a roll of toilet paper by her bed. "Damned if you're going to charge me $10 for a box of Kleenex," she tells the innocent cleaning staff every week.

"I'm almost finished packing. My plane leaves in the afternoon. If you think of something you need, call me and I can bring it in the morning," says Gina.

"I'm not worried about me, Gina. Just you. Something bothering you? Are you and Hal all right? I don't see much of him these days," says Bev and studies her daughter's face.

"Hal's been really busy. I haven't seen much of him either. He's not the visiting type, as you know." Gina wants to change the subject.

"So I know, but I also know you hate skiing and snow, so I wonder why you are going to spend all that money at a fancy ski resort."

"There are other things to do there. Shopping, spas, hiking."

"You hate all that too, and you're avoiding my question. What's going on?" Bev persists.

"The scenery is beautiful. Hal skis until it's dark. Hops in a sauna, has a drink or two, eats dinner, and goes to bed dog tired. He loves it."

"Umm, but you don't. Doesn't sound very romantic to me. Must be boring for you. How long can you look at overpriced bags and boots?" asks Bev.

"You know, Mother, I like to buy Christmas presents, cards, and even ornaments all year long. I can easily fill a day window-shopping. Maybe I can look for some new rims for your glasses. That sparkling leopard print is really dated. And, they're so dirty! Give them here."

Gina takes the glasses and gets her lens spritzer and cloth from her pocketbook. "Here. Maybe the world will look brighter now."

"Doubt that," says Bev. She examines her glasses before putting them on. "And, the nights? What do you do? Do you and Hal go out somewhere nice for dinner? Or, do you just sit around and watch Hal sleep?"

"The room has HBO, Showtime, Netflix, and the rest. So I catch up."

"You have that at home."

"Not for free," Gina says. "You could use some new slippers, too."

"Don't waste your money. These are almost new. See." Bev shows Gina the clean soles of her slippers. "Now, what is it? I can see it in your face. If it's bad news, I can handle it. I'm not a child, even though they treat me like a sick three-year-old in this place."

"It's not really bad news, not so bad anyway. I'm just not ready to talk about it." Gina looks at her hands and spins around her engagement ring and wedding band.

"Bad news is bad enough. Doesn't have to be badder. Well, I knew there was something. I guess I have to wait, but I don't like it."

Gina doesn't respond.

"So, where are you going? Vail?" Bev asks.

"Squaw Valley, Mother. Near Lake Tahoe. It's in California, but real close to Nevada."

"People break legs skiing." She warns Gina with her finger.

"Walking too, so use your cane." Gina picks it up from the floor and hands it to Bev. "Use it, please, for God's sake. Can't imagine how cheerful you'd be with a broken hip."

"Not funny. I hope you'll wear lots of sunscreen out there. Are you still using that pricey Clinique moisturizer? You need something for those lines around your eyes," Bev says, touching her own wrinkles. "Maybe that spa will have some better products."

"Thanks for mentioning my lines, Mother. I feel so much younger now."

"Well, I'm only saying what I see. Those lines on your forehead look new to me. Get some Frownies or whatever they're called," says Bev.

"Remember, Mother, I joined the AARP. So I got lines. I'm working on it."

"Well, you could do a better job. Stress, you know, makes wrinkles fast. But, don't go getting a facelift. You'll look worse after those butchers get through with you."

"Rhonda got one and she looks fabulous," says Gina.

"Rhonda? Lines weren't her only beauty problem."

"Oh, Mother, be nice."

"Nice I'm not. Gave that up when I moved in here. Wish I knew what you won't tell me, Gina. A mother knows when something's wrong."

"Knows what? I'm busy, that's all. Hal's busy. We both need a break."

"When are you leaving? Next week?" Bev asks.

"Tomorrow morning, remember? I won't see you again until I get back."

"Umm. Well, don't worry about me being here all alone. Rupert, next door, drops in, but he talks too much and always about himself. What am I? A tape recorder? God, I get tired of his life story."

"He's being thoughtful and nice, Mother, and so he talks about himself. We all do."

"You don't. You tell me nothing. He talks and talks, so much I feel I have to breathe for him. Won't stop until I tell him I have to go to the bathroom. Then, he pushes his walker away in a big hurry. He's going to fall flat on his face one of these days."

"Really, Mother. At least he tries. And, I do tell you things," says Gina. "All the time."

"Yeah, lots of nothings. New shoes, dishwasher broke, that stuff. I have no idea if you're happy, sad, or just bored. You keep everything to yourself and that's why you're getting those lines." Bev doesn't wait for Gina to interrupt. "You say everything's just great, but you look sad to me. I hope it's not Joey."

Gina shakes her head. "No, not Joey. Just got a lot on my mind today. Now be sure to take your pills. All of them. Look at this bottle. It's never been opened."

"Such a bore. Does Doctor Haynes really care if my blood pressure goes up five points or down ten? Does it matter? Pills, big, fat pills. That's all he offers."

"What do you want? There's no Fountain of Youth vaccination that I know of, but I can ask Dr. Haynes if he has one," Gina says and smiles at the thought.

Bev just shakes her head. "Some creative thinking would be nice. Or, some explanation why I have to take all these pills. Look at them! Just money makers for the drug companies. I'm old. Do they make that go away?"

"Of course not. Just makes being old feel better and with less pain," says Gina.

"Makes them feel better, you mean. You know they all own stock in those drug companies and we're putting their kids through college. It's not right," says Bev.

"Okay, don't get started on that. I've heard it all before, Mother. Many times. When I get back, I'll call Dr. Haynes and confirm all the pills you're supposed to be taking and why and when," Gina says.

Bev utters an "umm."

"Now, where am I going and when?" asks Gina.

"Vail. Tomorrow," says Bev with certainty.

"Mother! Not Vail. Squaw Valley in California, almost in Nevada. I've written it down on the pad on your desk, where, when, hotel number, flight numbers—all that. I also sent a copy to Aunt Cora and e-mailed it to Joey."

"Oh God. Now Cora'll be calling me every day." Bev sighs in resignation. "What's her dog's name?"

"Gypsy. Now, again. When am I leaving, where am I going?" Gina asks.

"You think I'm senile. Well, I'm not! That dog is all Cora talks about. Gypsy needs a haircut. Gypsy has fleas. Gypsy's got bad breath. Well, he's a damned dog, isn't he?"

"You love dogs."

"Yeah, but not all their owners," says Bev.

"You love Cora," Gina says.

"She's my only sister. Of course, I do. But, it's all Gypsy talk or the bad weather in Erie. It's Erie for God's sake. That hell hole," says Bev.

"Okay, Mother. I know you never wanted them to move there, but that's where Uncle Robert's job took him. They had to go."

"He's a lawyer. He could have found something around here? I know Cora hates Erie, and now I'll probably never see her again. Never." She looks out the window, not willing to show any sadness.

"Aunt Cora told me she might visit in the spring," says Gina.

"Don't believe it. She'll never travel alone and Robert won't budge except to see the Buffalo Bills."

"He has other vacation time," Gina says.

"Yeah, and they go to Florida to thaw out. Florida, the land of snowbirds, slow people, and blue plate specials. I couldn't stand it," says Bev.

"You could try, Go at the same time. I could put you on the plane and they'd meet you and you'd have a nice visit with some mild weather."

"Every time I've gone to Florida I froze. Even in Key West. TV told people to keep their pets indoors. Florida! And, then their politics!" Bev says as she waves them away.

"Let's not relive 2000 again, okay? It's over, forget it," Gina says with exasperation.

"Tell that to the Sub-Premes. So, what will you do in Lake Tahoe? See, I got it right this time."

"Almost. It's Squaw Valley to be precise. Shop. Go to the spa. Drink wine at lunch. Shop. Drink wine at dinner. Shop. Mother, are you napping?"

"No. Sometimes I just fake it. Especially when that Drumley woman stops by. I hope you're taking some good books, Gina. The stuff on TV is so vulgar. Predictable, too."

"I have my iPad. See." Gina takes it out of her bag to show Bev.

"I mean books. Real books. Like I read."

"They're too heavy to pack," says Gina. "There's a whole library in this thing."

Bev stares at it. "Didn't you want to give me one of those electronic miracles last Christmas?"

"You remember that?" asks Gina with surprise.

"And, I remember telling you to save your money. You're going to ruin your eyes. I want to turn paper pages."

"I really should go now," says Gina. She looks around to see if there's something else to do for her mother before she leaves and spots the laundry bag. "I'll return your laundry next week."

"Soon enough, no worry. Damned if they're going to charge me $20 a load."

Picking up the bag, Gina says, "Well, I saved the best for last, Mother. Here's some good news. Linda thinks she's pregnant."

"Thinks? Don't they do those drugstore tests these days? I thought—"

"She did that but wants her doctor to confirm it. She thinks she's about three months."

"Well, that is good news. Thank you, Gina, for telling me and not making me wait for it." Bev closes her eyes. "That'll make me a great grandmother! Never thought I'd live that long."

"And, I never doubted it," says Gina. "Take your pills and you might live even longer."

"I bet they're so happy. Joey will be a good, devoted father." She shakes her head yes, agreeing with herself. "Is Linda feeling all right? No problems?" Bev asks.

"She's throwing up a lot, morning sickness mostly, but it doesn't seem to bother her. Carries plastic bags with her to work and everywhere. She wants to keep working as long as she can."

Bev smiles. "I remember when you were pregnant with Joey and still working every day. Seemed like all you ate were saltines and even they came up. I was so worried. But you got over it." Bev looks out the window again. "Tell Linda it should stop soon and be sure to drink lots of water." She leans back in her recliner. "Imagine. Great grandmother."

Gina goes over to kiss her mother's cheek and bends down to give her a hug. This time Bev grabs her daughter's hands and says, "Don't worry about me. Take care of yourself and remember to wear sunscreen. Stress and sun will wrinkle your face. You don't want to look like an old grandmother, do you?" She smiles at her daughter. "Call me when you get there," she says and closes her eyes, ready for a nap.

Gina whispers "Love you lots" and leaves, walking quickly to avoid talking to anybody as she wipes away her tears. In her car, she opens the manila envelope she left on the passenger seat and pulls out her e-ticket to recheck the departure time for Reno-Lake Tahoe airport. Then she takes out the divorce papers, stapled, ready to be signed and witnessed. She reads the heading again. "Decree A Vinculo Matrimonii." A divorce from the bond of marriage was how her lawyer translated it. Remembering her Latin, Gina knows *vinculo* can also mean "chain." Chains plural would be more like it.

A Google site she once checked advertised Reno divorces for as low as $149. Quick too. Just fill out the papers online. They would even find you an apartment to satisfy the residency requirement. She wondered at the time what decent lawyer would go to Reno, stay there for six weeks, and obtain his own divorce? Now she knows. A cheap one in a hurry. Her Hal.

She thinks maybe she should have told her mother about Hal and his new love. She told Joey and made him promise not to tell his grandmother. But, how long would Bev remember it even if he did? The delayed news won't shock or sadden her, little does these days, and her mother always suspected Hal was unfaithful. At least she left her happy with the great grandchild announcement. Bev should remember that, Gina thinks. The not-so-bad news can wait.

An Ordinary Day

Lois M. Holden

(Honorable mention, Fralin Museum of Art Writers' Eye
contest, 2014; written on image by Gordon Parks, "Red
Jackson with His Mother and Brother, Harlem, New York,
1948," which can be viewed at
http://www.virginia.edu/artmuseum/pdf/WE2014/we2014-
selections.pdf, page 2)

On Thursdays we always had an early dinner because Momma
had choir practice at 7:30. After dinner, my brother and I
would clean the kitchen while Momma rested from her long
day at work.

This Thursday seemed a day like any other in April. As
I walked home from school, a brisk breeze brought a hint of
spring that was a welcome relief after the long winter. My mind
was on the history paper due after Easter vacation. I was a
good student and hoped to go to college. I was bound and
determined to get a good job and buy Momma a new house in
one of D.C.'s suburbs. Momma hoped my brother would
graduate high school and then enroll in college so he could get
a draft deferment. She was terrified he would be sent to Viet
Nam. James, however, cared nothing for school now. He'd
rather hang with his friends or go out with girls. He called me
"Einstein" and made jokes about my grades. Even though he
was three years older, he was only one grade ahead of me. His
eighteenth birthday was around the corner and he would be
eligible for the draft if he wasn't in school.

The wind gusted and I drew my sweater close around
me. Suddenly, an eddy of wind picked up a few pieces of paper
and several paper cups and deposited the trash at James' feet as
he leaned against a brick wall about half a block away. I
watched as the dust and paper swirled around him. He was
caught up in the whirlwind but didn't seem to realize it. His
only reaction was to turn his head and cup his hands around
his cigarette.

James and I used to be close, but he changed after our father's death in Viet Nam in 1966. When James was with his friends, I was invisible even though everyone knew we were brothers. As I passed him and his friends, I spoke to him anyway to remind him that it was Thursday. He ignored me, but I noticed that soon he was following me home.

Every evening Momma, James, and I would gather around our old black and white television to watch Walter Cronkite. He was the only news broadcaster Momma would watch—she trusted him to be unbiased in his reporting. That night, leaning against Momma's chair pretending to read, I was really thinking about a planned trip to New York City during Easter vacation. Momma had finally agreed that I could go with my friend Billy and his family. I had money saved from my summer job at the market. I had never traveled far from home and never without my mother. While I was excited about the trip, I was equally interested in spending time with Billy's sister, Joanna. She was fine! But she never looked twice at me.

Momma was reading her Bible passage for the day while waiting for the news to begin when James came in and sat on the arm of her chair, a cigarette dangling from his mouth.

"James, get away from me with that cigarette. You know I hate that smoke."

"Okay, Momma, but let me have a couple of dollars for tonight," James asked. This was a nightly ritual with them. James always asked and Momma always refused. I never knew where he got his cigarette money, much less money for his girlfriends.

"You're not going anywhere tonight. This is Thursday. You stay home with your brother. And you'd better be home when I get back. Now hush up. I want to hear the news. Dr. King is back in Memphis today. I'm afraid there's going to be more trouble over that strike."

After the news, Momma sighed, put on her coat, and left for the church. She walked to choir practice, meeting up with friends on the way. I know they talked about all the neighbors. She left at seven on the dot, not wanting to miss out on any of the good gossip and making sure she wasn't the topic of discussion.

James left right after Momma. "You know she'll be late tonight. They'll be practicing their Easter program. I'll be home before nine."

I went to my bedroom that I shared with James and started working my history paper. I didn't want to have to worry about it while I was in New York.

About eight o'clock, Momma burst in through the front door with Aunt Tirzah close behind. "James, John! Come here quick. Oh, Lord, Lord!"

"What's the matter, Momma? Are you okay?" I could see fear in her eyes and tears running down Aunt Tirzah's face.

"Where's James? Jesus, Lord. That boy will be the death of me. Where is he?"

"I don't know, Momma. He left right after you did. He said he'd be home by nine. What is the matter with you?"

"You don't know? How could you not know? Haven't you been watching the TV?"

"No, Momma. I've been working on that paper for school."

"Turn the TV on and be quick. They've shot Dr. King! Deacon Johnson came in and told us at rehearsal. Where is James? There's going to be trouble. I just know it."

As she said those words, I felt my world shift on its axis.

The TV finally warmed up and we saw Walter Cronkite's face instead of the regular program. Reports started coming in about the riots in D.C. Momma sat up real straight, grabbed my hand and started crying. "James. Oh, James. Where are you? Please come home."

But James didn't come home that night or any other night. He was killed by glass from a storefront window or so his friends said. Momma just sat in her chair after that blankly staring at the wall. She never recovered from his death.

My world did shift that night. Nothing was ever the same. Not after that ordinary, extraordinary April day. April 4, 1968.

A Slow Spring Music

Erin Newton Wells

(First place fiction, *Skyline* spring contest, 2015)

The clamor becomes too much. At their best, a group of bells can be a marvelous cohesion, honeyed and seamless. In ordinary hands they are so much brass, splashed with vinegar. I come to the decision both suddenly and slowly, traveling here all my life. Finally I tell them. It is an awkward place to stop.

Already they are well into the big events of spring, rehearsing for Easter. Forsythia has bloomed. Dogwood begins. But I know what I must do. It is a matter of listening for interior music. When I hear it unmistakably, it is time to tell them and not look back.

"But you can't," says Hilde, who stands to my left. "You're the anchor."

"We need you," says Diane, who stands to my right. "You're tempo. You're the beat."

"There will be others," I tell them. "The beat will find you. All is well."

And I depart in peace.

From now on I will be quiet and slow. I will sing, if the songs are good. If not, I will be quiet. I will sing to myself. I will make harmony for the tunes, singing a lonely alto in the dark at night or when I work outside. Then I will cease and let the song continue on its own. That is when the music knows exactly what to do.

Hilde calls several times, distraught, urging my return.

"Don't worry," I say. "Let someone new try. Wait and see."

I imagine the long, padded tables, the brass bells lined in swelling rows from teashop tiny to enormous buckets. In the middle is the gap where I stand. My spirit hovers over it, keeping tranquillity. Others scurry to fill in when my notes appear on the page.

And then I imagine the piece played without my bells, an empty space at those notes, brief silences. The silence spreads slowly left and right beneath their playing, a hushed substance that calms them. It is mellow, smooth, round, a warm and melting gold that curls into the ear, gives comfort and no pain.

Hank's gone, so there's just me. And in the afternoons there's Lollie. To most, I am Merle. To her, I am Moom, a name she formed for me when her small mouth was soft and new. It could not bend around sounds that take place farther back. She is so fresh and malleable, a chance to start over.

I walk to the school now to fetch her, as I've done each weekday this year. It helps Kate. She picks her up around five after work. It saves on childcare, better for Lollie. I get another chance to pass along what I know and maybe do some good. Such a messy divorce. In earlier times we kept it hidden and soldiered on. Who's to say? The little ones bounce around more when the halves split.

Here she comes, skipping to the gate, and halts with the line of children. Security is fierce. Gone are the days when children walked home on their own, as Kate did. Now they are checked off to a recognized adult, the time marked, their small lives burdened early.

She spots me and raises her hand. I raise mine, the required salute. The aide scrutinizes me, smiles, lets Lollie through the gate. A sheep from the fold returns to my imperfect arms. Oh, Lollie, I think. I will surround you with simplicity these two hours each day, as long as I can.

"Moom!" Her small body hits me with a thud.

"Sweet Lollie!" I exclaim. I wrap myself around her, miniature backpack and all.

I am ancient among these late-model parents, the pitch of their voices still high, their faces fresh.

She shrugs out of the pack and hands it to me. Already it is too full. She is only six. I try to spare her back. The bag is custom stitched with her name and a stylized lollipop. "In case you forget it's me," she explains on the first day of school. So far, this has worked. I slip into the straps, gingerly easing them over an achy shoulder. It is a reminder of when I first began playing bells and did not use the proper oval motion. Now and then the left joint flares. You are mortal, it says, and flawed.

"I missed you!" she says.

"That makes two of us, because I missed you, too."

"All day?"

"Every second."

She grins and begins to skip, tugging my hand. The metal parts of the lunchbox inside the pack clank and whump against me as we sail coltishly past the young mothers and dads. The grass fluoresces with its first green. Everything is April new.

"What will we do today, Moom?" she asks.

"What do you think?" I turn the question back, good Sophoclean form.

"Let's gather something."

"Good idea. Snack first."

"Fuel for the journey." She repeats a phrase I use.

Gather is not a typical word for a six-year-old, or journey. But I have begun to enfold her with my odd, outdated speech. I smile to hear myself speaking from her small face. We often embark upon gathering journeys together.

"And what shall we gather, my fair young maid?" I sing. She giggles, which also happens frequently.

"Dewberries!"

"Ah. Would that we could. But too early for them. Not until summer."

She skips in her one-footed version, galump, galump, as she thinks.

"Let's search for the rare, perfect leaf of spring."

My heart leaps to hear this baby conversing in Elizabethan.

"Your wish is granted. Rare and perfect it is. Plenty of those where I live."

We pass the young dogwoods the school planted. They've just begun to bloom. Lollie stops.

"Look, Moom! Someone hurt them. Every petal."

We examine what appear to be burn marks on the ends of each white heart, and I say this is how they grow. Later, I will tell her the legend.

We move down the quiet street leading to my house. We stop to watch ants, squirrels, rocks, broken nut shells, a redbud frothed with mauve blooms. How compelling is this world the lower you are to the ground. I am in no hurry. There's time.

She finishes snack and is soon out the door again, pulling me with her. She's grabbed our floppy and misshapen journey hats from their hooks and adds the two good hickory branches we found out back. They are slender and resilient, stripped of bark and silky smooth.

Our property is large, extending a good distance back, a lot of it useless except for adventures. It's old farm land redone as subdivision. We head through the Bramble Briers, the Wild Ivy Patch, the Stone Gnome Homes, the Poor Dead Animal Place, which is the graveyard for Kate's childhood pets. Lollie has named all this.

She remembers our mission and slows to examine leaves, looking for the rare and perfect. I can see many. But she is quite particular.

"No," she says, pointing to infinitely small deformities on each one.

By now we've reached the back of the wooded lot, beginning to be shaded again as trees fill out. It contains the old culvert from the farm road that ran through here, draining the land when it rains. It used to be fenced, but all of that rusted and fell away. The place is a hazard, and Frank was going to fix it. Lollie knows to be careful. She knows how far she can go.

I see her heading there but keep quiet. They are so protected these days. Let her experiment. I move closer, ready.

"Moom!" I see it!" She points into the hole. "It's beautiful! Come see!"

Instantly I am beside her as she squats to show me a lovely yellow-green leaf of a sapling that grows through the cracked wall of the drain. It rained yesterday. The concrete is wet, streaked with mud. Right here the pipe goes straight down, then levels out. It's an overgrown mess.

"It's perfect!" she says. "I can reach it, okay?" She holds out her hand to me for support.

Alarms go off inside me. I extend my hand. She grips it. Her feet are straining at the edge, her other hand reaching for the leaf. She slips. I hear her smack the puddle of muddy water.

68

"Lollie! Oh, baby!"

What on earth was I thinking? She lies on her back and looks up at me, her eyes huge.

"Baby, are you broken? Can you move? Did you hit your head? Speak, honey."

"Moom?" A tiny voice. Her lip quivers.

"Are you hurt, baby?"

"I got my school clothes all muddy." She examines an elbow. "And this is all scrapey."

"We can fix that. Are you able to move around?"

She sits up and nods.

"Good. Then just stay there while we think."

"Moom? I'm scared. I don't like it down here."

"Can't say I blame you."

"I'm all wet and icky. Can you get me out?"

"I will. But you're a bit too far to reach. I'd slide down, too. Then we'd both be in a pickle."

"You could use the journey stick."

We'd talked about rescuing people this way when they fell into water. But with my bum shoulder, I'm not sure I can pull her up. The sides of the drain are too slick for her to scramble out on her own. I test the reach of the stick, but I'm afraid I'll drop her and make it worse. I look around for someone else, but I know the neighbors aren't likely to be home now.

"Lollie, I can go check next door for help."

"No, Moom! Don't leave me," she moans.

"All right." I sit on the edge where she can see me.

People are always leaving her. First, her Big Frank Pops. He loved that little girl, and the feeling was mutual. Then, her father. That left a big hole. She's been dropped off at daycare and now, these past two years, at school. This year, there's no dad to pick her up, and mom needs to work more hours. That's where I come in. My real purpose in life right now, I've decided, is not to be absent for Lollie. She still clutches the leaf.

"Looks like you got a good one," I say.

She grips it more tightly.

"You still okay?"

She's quiet. Then, "I'm scared, Moom." Tiny voice.

"Well, who wouldn't be, in a predicament like this? But I suppose it's all for a reason. We just have to figure out what."

She considers this. I can see her face thinking.

"Like it's our journey?"

I brighten. "Exactly. What a brilliant child you are. You already found the perfect leaf of spring. That was the first part. Now we just have to figure out this second part."

I lie down and stretch out.

"Moom?" she says nervously.

"I'm still here." I edge over so she sees more of me.

"What are you doing?"

"Looking at the sky."

"Why?"

"Because it makes me feel peaceful. Try it."

I hear her rustling. Then she's still. Softly I start singing her name to a wandering tune. I add words that rhyme with it. Polly, holly, jolly, kabolly. I make them up. She giggles, joins in. When we run out, she sings my name, then makes rhymes. The sky glides calmly overhead. I'm silent.

"Moom?"

"I'm listening to my interior music."

"What's that?"

"If I let everything go quiet in me, sometimes I start to hear a slow little tune inside."

She's quiet.

"I don't hear it."

"It takes time. You may have to wait awhile. But it's there."

"Inside everybody?"

"Yes."

She's quiet.

"Moom? What was your name when you were a little girl?"

"Same as now. Merle. Until you came along. Then I became Moom, too. But I'm still Merle. You could call me Moom Merle."

She giggles.

"What was your name before you were Lollie?"

"Shaneesy," she says, without hesitation.

"Ah. Your angel name."

"Huh?"

"Before you were born. When you were an angel."

"Oh. Yes. That's what it was. What was your angel name?"

"Nell. I'm pretty sure. It's been so long ago."

"You're Merle Nell?"

"I think it's Nell Merle, since Nell came first. Nell Merle Moom. That would be the right order."

She giggles. I do, too. The name sounds like a cheer. Sis Boom Bah. We laugh until our middles hurt.

"Silly Moom! I mean Nell Merle Moom!"

"Shaneesy Lollie Holly Polly!"

Then she's quiet.

"I miss who I was when I was born," she says.

"Why?"

"Because Daddy would've been there. And I'd get to see him all the time."

I take a deep breath.

"I miss Daddy. I miss Big Frank Pops."

"So do I."

"Pops isn't coming back, is he?"

"No, Lollie."

The other question hangs in the air. I begin to sing all the angel names I can think of to fill up the space.

"Moom?"

"Still here."

"Don't leave me."

"Never."

We're quiet. She's lying on the soggy blue hat, her brown hair spread out.

"I hear it," she says.

"Good girl. What's it sound like?"

"It goes slow."

I don't correct the adverb.

"I like it. I think it's the angels. Like what I used to be."

There's a thought. We close our eyes and listen.

71

Then I hear something crashing through the brush on the slope, and here's Hank, our neighbor, standing beside me. Hank and Frank, I called them. Like two old housewives out in the yard, keeping up with whatever they kept up with.

"Merle!" he yells. Hank is hard of hearing. "You hurt?"

"Hi, Hank. What took you so long? Maybe you could give us a hand."

"I just got back, looked over, saw you lying flat out here. You all right?"

He reaches for me, but I brush him off and stand, putting my hat back on.

"Let's get Lollie out." I take him to look.

"Goodness, gracious, young lady! You okay?"

"Hi, Mr. Hank."

"Well, honey, I'm going to get you out there right now, don't you worry."

I suggest he use the stick, but he'll have none of it. He hustles off, comes back with a rope, which he ties to a tree, then dangles into the pipe.

"Now you come over to the side, darling. Grab a hold tight. I'm going to walk you up the side till I can reach, then I'll pull you rest of the way. Think you're strong enough? You eat your vegetables today?"

She nods in amazement.

"Then it ought work."

He coaxes her up, her sneakers braced on the side, with me holding the rope behind him.

"Ready now? Keep hanging on, both you young ladies."

When she's within reach, he grabs her, lifts her out, and starts to the house, carrying her like a baby.

"Moom!" she cries. "I forgot my leaf!"

"Sweetheart," I call, jogging to keep up with Hank. "It's still perfect, no matter where it is. It's still spring. There's plenty more to find."

He places her, mud and all, on the sofa and waits to make sure she's okay.

"Going out right now, get that fencing like me and Frank was set on. Should've done it. Aimed to fix it come spring."

"Go for it, Hank. I'll pay."

"We'll see about that."

I get things to clean her, and an old shirt of mine for a dress, a bandage for the scraped elbow.

"Well, then," I say. "I guess that counts as an adventure."

"But could we not do that one again, Moom?"

"Well, if we did, you'd know how to handle it."

She nods. "I get quiet and listen to my angels."

It took me a whole lifetime to learn that. Here she is, only in first grade.

It's nearly five. The phone rings. Hilde tries to persuade me I should come to practice tonight. I remind her how she and Diane can two-in-hand the bells for awhile, taking my part until they find a replacement. I tell her I need to step aside now.

"But you're coming back, after that?"

I say I've got other music I need to listen to.

"Merle. You're not switching to that group at St. Stephen's, are you?"

I laugh, assure her I'm not.

"Moom?" Lollie asks when I hang up. "You're not going to your handbells tonight?"

"No, dear."

"You'll stay with me?"

"Ever and ever."

The phone rings. It's Kate, saying she's running late, apologizing. I tell her it's my greatest privilege to keep Lollie a little longer, that we're engaged in some serious music.

"Okay, then. Everything go all right this afternoon?"

"The afternoon was perfect," I say, giving Lollie a conspiratorial look. "In fact, why don't you just let her stay here overnight. I'll get her to school in the morning."

Lollie gives a whoop, rushes to hug me. Nothing obvious is broken in her. I hand her the phone so she can talk to her mother. I see Hank backing into my driveway and

73

unloading bales of fence wire and bundles of metal posts. Lollie is explaining the name Shaneesy, as if her mother ought to know this.

I go to the kitchen to start supper, selecting things that might please angels. The tune inside is slow, definitely about spring, because it grows more beautiful, more perfect with time.

The Truth

(Honorable mention, Fralin Museum of Art Writers' Eye
contest, 2014; written on image by Gordon Parks, "untitled,
Harlem, New York, 1948," which can be viewed at
http://www.virginia.edu/artmuseum/pdf/WE2014/we2014-
selections.pdf, page 2, top row, photograph on right)

Maybe you saw it. Could have been looking out the window
right then. Well, that was me. Just my head, trying to stay out
of the way. I'm only ten. You know?

That day, wished I'd stayed all the way home, inside like
where you were. Like Big Mama tells me. She's my grandma.
You meet her, you won't forget. She's got The Truth. That's
what she calls it. This time, I don't know.

I take off to the schoolyard, maybe shoot some hoops.
Nobody's got a real ball to play with. Jump up, shoot that air
ball. Hahhh! Yeah. Smack it right in. Maybe some friends come
by and we get up a game.

On my way I see these two big guys hogging the
sidewalk. I know who they are. We all do. They got mean
blades. So I say to myself, Be small. I scooch up next the
building, far as I can get in the shadow.

They own this street. The Sharps. Try to own me, too,
Big Mama says. She says stay clear of them. But she's not out
here all the time like me. She's got The Truth. But maybe it's
the inside kind of truth.

They keep circling, fists up, itching for that first move.
Saying things you ought not hear. Street's cleared out. Nobody
wants a taste of that. I keep back.

Then I hear something, quiet like, breathing right next
to me. I nearly jump out my skin. Another big guy is standing
in the doorway beside me. I know him, too. He's one of them.

I tell myself, You're gone now, little bud. End of the
line for you.

But he stands there, arms crossed, breathing so quiet.
Then he makes this move of the hand, like, get back. So I do.

Flat up against the wall. Try to look like a brick. I don't breathe. He gives this quick smile and nods. Whew! I'm still on the train.

We stand there, those guys about to kill each other, when one looks up. Just that minute my head comes part way out the shadow? I don't know. But he sees me and yells. You don't want to hear what. Stops beating on the other and comes my way. I see me in one of those nice coffins they get up to the church. Big Mama crying her eyes out. I think, This is it, and I'm only ten.

But this quiet guy steps in front of me, pushes me behind so none of me shows. He stands there so still, breathing.

Angry guy yells out things about me and the quiet one, more of what you don't want to know. My ears are burning off. But this guy? He just stands there, arms crossed. How's he stay so calm? I'd scream if my mouth would move. But I'm like one of those bricks. I don't twitch.

Angry guy takes a swipe at my guy. My guy reaches back, pushes me, says, "Scoot."

Man, no need to say it twice. I scoot like a rabbit, so fast you don't see. But when I get far enough I turn and look back. Angry guy pounds my guy. My guy pounds back, and I see blood on his shirt. I don't know who it's from. That third guy's laughing like it's a big joke. I see him flick open a blade. I try to say a prayer for the quiet one, but it comes out all mush.

Back home Big Mama says, "Where you been, Baby?"

I tell her to the schoolyard. The truth. I just don't tell what's on the way. I step all around the middle. I can't lie to Big Mama. You know?

But her eyes say, What is your mouth not speaking? She reads me plain as a schoolbook on my face. I don't sleep much that night. Would you?

Next day she sits me down, gives me breakfast, and lets me eat. But she keeps watching and I'm about to choke. Then she tells me what she heard this morning from old Miss Claudie next door on the landing. A ruckus down to the schoolyard yesterday.

"About the time you go there, Baby." She looks at me hard. "Somebody near your size who ought not be there. Comes right along into all that. But one of those young toughs stands up for him, keeps him back of it. You know what happened?"

I shake my head.

"The one protecting that little one? His eye got busted. Lost it for good. Half of him can't see now."

I can't breathe.

"If somebody do that for you, you'd be in his debt your whole life. Not to the bad part of how he is. That's still wrong. But to the good part, the angel part. Look at me, Baby."

And here it comes, like I told you.

"All this I say? It's The Truth. There's only one. Not two. You got to follow just that one. Sometimes it gets all mixed up with the other. But the good one, the angel part? You stick with that."

She nods her head, begins to clear the table. Breakfast is a square, solid block in my throat.

"Go on to school now, Baby."

I get my books, and she hands me a lunch. It'll just be stolen. But I take it, like I always do.

She pulls me over and kisses me on the head.

"Not easy, Baby. But it's The Truth. You think on it. In here." She pounds her big, soft chest, where the heart is.

I let myself out the door and down the steps, closing first one eye, then the other. Then opening both. I see one thing. Then I don't. I see another. Which eye you look from keeps changing it. How you going to find the truth this way? So I'd like to know what you saw.

Stella by Starlight

Elizabeth Doyle Solomon

(Second place fiction, *Skyline* spring contest, 2015)

Estelle first saw him on the baseball field in their little neighborhood park. He was batting for the St. Claude Angels—trim, muscular, a twinkle in his green eyes even at this distance from the bleachers. She elbowed her friend, Gerry. "Who is *that* good-looking batter for the Angels?"

Gerry handed the popcorn bag to Estelle before she answered. "Honey, you don't want to mess with *him*! He's a lady-killer for sure!"

Estelle sipped her soda and stared at Mr. Handsome, who had just scored a home-run. She and Gerry stood up to cheer. "All right, Angels!" they shouted with the St. Claude crowd. "His name is Carroll, with two *r*'s and two *l*'s. When he turns around, look at the name on his shirt." Gerry pointed, "Now!—See? Carroll Johnson." Estelle stared, already a bit in love.

"Why did you say he's a lady-killer, Gerry? And how do you know that anyway?" Estelle took a lipstick and mirror from her purse and applied a little more "Hot Pink Passion." Her shoulder-length blonde hair fell in lovely waves, framed a peaches-and-cream complexion. Large blue eyes looked questioningly at Gerry. "You see that cute redhead in the popcorn stand? She was his latest disaster. Fell head over heels for him about a year ago. Took a 'sudden' trip to see an old aunt in Florida and came back nine months later. Everybody knew it was Carroll's baby she gave up for adoption."

Estelle shook her head slowly. "I don't believe in gossip and neither should you, Gerry!" The crowd was standing, hooting for the Angels, who had scored again over the Galvez Street Saints. That was New Orleans for you: a largely Catholic city dominated by saints and angels—both in and out of its churches.

"This game is almost over, and the Angels have it wrapped up. Come on, Gerry—you introduce me to him in the dugout." Gerry's face frowned beneath a curly mop of black hair. "OK, Estelle Fisher, but you'd better be *careful!*"

The eighteen-year-old friends wiggled their firm young bodies through bleachers' crowds with all the vigor and excitement of foolish youth. Estelle and Gerry had met in St. Mary's kindergarten and became close in the first week of school. They stayed best friends—through measles, mumps, chickenpox, and Sister Rose Marie's horrible fifth grade. After eighth-grade graduation, they both enrolled in the all-girls Holy Angels Academy and finished their senior year together. Freedom had never felt so good as now, their smooth young legs tanned and bare below shorts just tight enough to be decent.

"Hey, Carroll!" Gerry called down to the dugout of the Angels, who were patting each other on the back and shaking hands. Gerry whispered quickly to Estelle, "You be careful, girl!" They felt the team's excitement of victory, their own cheeks flushing bright with a mixture of pride and girlish hormones.

Carroll Johnson was even more of a knockout at close range: black hair; eyes green as emeralds; handsome square-jawed face, cleft right in the center of his chin; good tan. "Carroll, this is my best friend Estelle. She's been cheering for you!"

Carroll reached for Estelle's hand and squeezed it, and she felt electric tingles all the way up her arm. Estelle nodded, her tongue stuck like glue in her mouth. Gerry answered, "Yeah—from St. Mary's kindergarten all the way through to graduation at Holy Angels."

Estelle retrieved her tongue. "Where did *you* go to school, Carroll?"

He gave Estelle one of his "knock-'em-dead" smiles. "I went to St. Anthony's on Canal Street, then DeLaSalle until the tenth grade. But I had to drop out." He stopped abruptly, as if some inner pain was too deep to continue. "It's OK, though. I got a fantastic job with Coca-Cola. The plant manager was a DeLaSalle boy himself."

People were thinning and clearing out of the park. Fireflies began twinkling on-off, on-off in the late spring night.

Carroll asked, "How's about a root beer float? You girls have any other plans?"

Gerry gave him a quick smile and shook her black curls. "I can't do it tonight, Carroll—promised Aunt Lou I'd babysit my niece. She and Uncle Rick are going to a movie. Why don't *you* go with him, Estelle?"

Carroll's green eyes were going over Estelle, head to toe. "What do you say, Estelle?" She blushed and the effect was beautiful to see, red roses on her cheeks. "Gee," he said, "you look pretty when you blush!"

Estelle mumbled a thank you and told him she'd love a root beer float.

Gerry took off with a wave and left the pair together. And that's how it all started, how Estelle Fisher fell absolutely head over heels in love with Carroll Johnson. They were married three months later by a justice of the peace on Claiborne Avenue. Estelle did not discover until after she married Carroll that his father had been a lifelong alcoholic. His daily bar trips bankrupted the family, and Carroll had to leave DeLaSalle. There was no money for Catholic school tuition, and nearly no money for food. They moved to subsidized housing, and soon afterward Carroll's father committed suicide with an overdose of his wife's prescription pain pills.

Estelle took her wedding vows seriously, especially after Carroll Jr. was born. It was a difficult birth, and the doctor confirmed that she could not risk another pregnancy. Gerry, of course, had been right in her appraisal of Carroll. He had many flirtations that led to affairs. Estelle knew about them all, the heavily made-up girls who followed his baseball games. He was also a heavy drinker like his father.

When little Carroll was three years old, Estelle thought that if she and her husband sanctified their marriage in a Catholic ceremony, maybe he would sober up, leave the women alone, maybe *also* treat her better. A priest at St. Anthony's performed the ceremony. Estelle even wore a bridal dress and veil and asked her sisters Odette and Selma to be bridesmaids.

Carroll's demeanor softened at first toward Estelle after the ceremony. She was, after all, startling—beautiful, sweet, with an infectious laugh that made everyone around her laugh too. But his good moods did not last. Abusive language turned to abusive slaps and punches. Odette and Selma saw the bruises, knew the story. They pleaded with her to leave. "Come and bring little Carroll with you, Estelle," Selma begged. "Mike and I don't have any children yet."

But Estelle would not leave him. "He's still so good to me at times," she explained. "He calls me his 'Stella By Starlight.' And who would take care of him? He *needs* me."

Gerry went often to see Estelle and her son—but only when big Carroll was not home. When Gerry saw a puffy black eye on her friend's face, she knew what Estelle's decision had cost her. Estelle never learned to drive, so she was completely dependent on her husband for groceries, doctors, and church. Carroll Junior left home as soon as he graduated high school. He, too, only visited Estelle when his father was gone. That was easy now, because of an accident in the Coca-Cola truck that caused a permanent disability. Carroll no longer worked but left every morning at 9:00 a.m. for a local bar and returned home every afternoon at 2:00 p.m. to sleep off his stupor.

Estelle never faltered in her devotion to him. She had his dinner ready every evening, washed his clothes, and kept the house spotless. In return for this devotion, Carroll became apathetic, almost as if to say, "Well, if she's that stuck on me, I guess I don't even have to be nice to her anymore." He stopped driving her to buy groceries or to the doctor's office. He refused to attend church with her. "Just a bunch of false idols, those statues." He would sputter and curse the good intentions of nuns and priests.

Estelle had no choice but to take city transit. She had to transfer twice to the doctor's office. St. Anthony's was two buses, and then a trolley. She struggled with bags of groceries on the difficult trips back home. When Carroll Junior found out, he was furious. "Why do you put up with him, Mom?"

Estelle gave the same tired answer that she gave to her sisters and to Gerry. "I feel sorry for him, honey."

In her fiftieth year, Estelle's hands and feet began to swell with often-unbearable pain. Arthritic nodules appeared on all her joints, especially fingers, elbows, and ankles.

"What does the doctor say, Mom?" her son asked on a rainy November day after he had driven her to the specialist's office on St. Charles Avenue. He was an immunologist, a doctor who had spent his career studying why some patients' illnesses did not respond to their bodies' own immune systems.

"He's not sure, Carroll. But these new pills seem to take most of the pain away." She showed him the receipt from the drugstore. $65 for a month's supply.

"I'm sure Daddy doesn't give a damn how you pay for these!" Carroll shouted.

Estelle began to cry. "He's all crippled up himself, honey. I manage."

Carroll held his mother as though she were a child. "Listen, Mom. I have a great job now as a computer programming manager. You know I make good money. You will *not* pay a penny more from your house money for medicine. I know Daddy has no medical coverage for either of you. Now don't you worry. As long as I live, I'll take care of you."

Estelle was diagnosed with Lou Gehrig's Disease twelve years later. She was sixty-two. Carroll Junior was true to his word. He paid for all her medicine, got her on disability and Medicaid, which paid for home nursing care. When Gerry visited her with a cake for her sixty-fifth birthday, she was wheelchair bound. She still had her girlish figure, and her blue eyes smiled with joy to see her old friend. They talked of long-ago days, their school terms at St. Mary's and Holy Angels.

An aging Carroll walked in, drunk as always, before Gerry left. "Well, would you look who's here? How are ya, Gerry girl?" His words were slurred, and he reeked of alcohol.

"*Look* at Estelle, Carroll!" Gerry raised her voice so that Carroll had to pay attention. "She's *always* in pain. She's in a wheelchair and she *still* cooks your supper! Aren't you ashamed of yourself?"

Carroll flopped down in his recliner chair a little too hard. "Aw, Gerry. Estelle's fine, pretty as ever. My 'Stella By

Starlight.' I love her much as ever, like that first day when I batted for the Angels and we won the game. Nothing much wrong with her—she's just getting old, like me!"

Carroll rambled on in a babble and fell asleep in his chair. Gerry kissed her old friend. "Now Estelle, I filled the refrigerator and freezer with precooked stuff. All you need to do is microwave them, honey." She hurried out the door, afraid that Estelle would see the tears brimming in her eyes.

In two years Estelle's doctor had ordered Hospice care for her. She was sixty-seven. Everyone thought this was surely the end, but the old sweet Estelle also had a stubborn streak. When the parish priest came from St. Anthony's every week to give her Communion, she told him, "God's not ready for me yet, but the doctors don't know that." She smiled at the old priest who had married her and Carroll all those years ago. "I'm going to hold on a bit longer until my angel comes for me." She winked and a smile lit the suffering blue eyes.

Estelle died in her sleep on the eve of her seventieth birthday. Gerry and Estelle's sisters, Odette and Selma, attended the funeral Mass at St. Anthony's church. Carroll Junior was a pall bearer, but that handsome old ballplayer, husband and father, was too drunk to attend.

In an almost uncanny justice, Hurricane Katrina struck New Orleans with its own vengeance three years after Estelle was laid to rest. The small "shotgun" house she had shared with Carroll for nearly fifty-two years filled to the rafters with raging flood waters. Some folks were swept away. Others waited on rooftops or from high-rise windows to be rescued by Coast Guard helicopters. Estelle's sister, Selma, was one of these. Deposited at the Convention Center, she waited in boiling sun for two days while useless school buses filled with lake waters. Gerry caught up with Selma after a nephew transported her to Houston. "Whatever happened to Estelle's husband?" she asked.

Selma cursed under her breath and answered, "He's probably been drowned, and surely in hell for how he treated my sister."

Gerry drove to the devastated house where Estelle had taken her final breath. There was a huge red X painted on the front door, meaning no body had been found inside. She asked around in the few houses where owners had returned to salvage and start over. No one ever knew, either, what had happened to the son who had been so devoted to his mother.

Among the old neighbors who had known Estelle and Carroll Johnson, all agreed that she was a saint. "That sweet, blue-eyed little blonde—what she endured all those years. But she never said a word against him!"

Gerry continued to put flowers on Estelle's grave in the cemetery at the end of Canal Street, every year on the anniversary of her death. It was she who ordered and paid for an engraving on the mausoleum's door:

> Estelle Fisher Johnson   1922–2002
> "You're an angel in the night,
> our Stella by Starlight."

Midnight

Brenda A. Morris

The moon was still low in the sky and the house was filled with deep, dark, iced tea shadows when I woke. I heard the dogs out back, their chains clanking as they moved. I listened to my daughter breathing beside me and closed my eyes again.

Then Jill called a single beagle belling call. I hoped it was a fox prancing across the field that woke her. But it wasn't, for then I heard the crunch of tires on rocks as the car came creeping down the long driveway. Not again, I prayed.

When the car was within sight of the house, both dogs began to call, warning the driver to stop. The car kept coming. When it reached the edge of the yard, it finally stopped and sat, engine running and lights off.

Suddenly a fiddle's screech from the radio split the night. My daughter woke screaming.

"It's okay," I said, pulling her into my arms.

The music blared. The dogs bayed. Song followed song and Robin drifted back to sleep. The absence of sound is as loud as its presence. With the silence Robin woke again. The dogs, Robin, and I all waited. Usually at this point the car would leave. Tonight was different. The car's engine roared and light flooded the night. Tires crushed rocks as the car gathered speed. A single pistol shot ripped the fabric of the night, and Robin screamed again. Light swept over the house and then away as the car went around the circular driveway, like some moving lighthouse beacon. The dogs were going wild.

"I want Daddy," Robin sobbed in my arms.

I said nothing.

"Doesn't he love us anymore?"

I sighed. "He loved you very much, but he's angry right now and sometimes when someone is really angry they do crazy things."

"Then tell him to stop being angry and come back to being my daddy! Tell him to make these men stop coming here!"

I held her close, stroking her hair. I wish I could, I said to myself. But he was probably driving that car out there.

Win, Win

Olivia Stowe

(From *Spirit of Christmas*)

I pursed my lips as I stood outside Corey's bedroom door and listened to his evening prayers.

". . . . and Shady our cat, and . . . and . . . make me win when we play the Tigers tomorrow afternoon."

I thought I'd drummed into Corey better than that that praying to win games was neither a good use of God or a sign of good sportsmanship. I was wavering there, wondering if I should go in right now to talk to him and reveal that I had been eavesdropping or try to bring the subject up the next day, when I tuned into what he then prayed for.

". . . . and make Tom win too, please. He's not as good at baseball as I am, and so he needs to win real bad."

All right, then, I thought, as I pulled away from the door. He had moved on to more selfless requests. But Corey's prayers were pretty impossible to satisfy, even for God. Tom was on the Tigers' baseball team. It was getting close to the end of the season and Corey's team was a contender for the championship. They certainly wouldn't take even a tie with a basement-level team like the Tigers as any sort of win even if it still gave them the championship. There would be the bad taste in their mouths of losing to a basement team that would haunt them until the next season.

Still, it was heartening to know that Corey was concerned for the unfortunate Tom. The two had been the unlikeliest of best friends, coming, as they did, from two entirely different worlds, and Corey being blest in academic and sports talent in almost diametrical opposition to all of Tom's unsuccessful strivings. But their friendship had survived, and even had flourished, through their kindergarten and elementary school years.

The afternoon of the baseball game proved quite surprising and not a little frustrating for Tom's team, as the Tigers—despite all the help that Tom's erstwhile fumbling at bat and in the outfield was giving Corey's team—were holding their own in the score. It was the bottom of the ninth, with the Tigers at bat and only one run down. For the first time that afternoon, though, Corey's team was pretty confident, because they had two outs and the ideal batter stood between the end of the game and the Tigers' best two sluggers. That batter, of course, was Tom, who hadn't connected with a ball, on either offense or defense, all afternoon.

If the Tigers had a clever coach, of course, this would have been the time to bring in a pinch hitter, but if their coach had been at all clever, they probably wouldn't have been in the league cellar to begin with. He left a trembling Tom standing, wobbling knees, at home plate, the weight of the game on his shoulders.

Watching from his third-base position, Corey's eyes filled with tears from concern for his friend, and he stumbled out another prayer—a prayer that the Tigers' coach would take Tom off the batter's plate before he was totally humiliated. But nothing of the sort happened.

As always, Tom closed his eyes tight and swung wildly at the first pitch. This is what Tom always did—he closed his eyes and fanned at all of the pitches. But this time something unusual happened. His bat connected with the ball—not solidly and not with any force on the ball, so that it slowly hopped, skipped, and jumped between first and second bases rather than soared for the fences. And it came up dead about halfway out toward right field.

Normally the ball would have been fielded easily, but everyone on the field, including Tom, was so surprised that he'd actually hit the ball at all, that everyone stopped dead in shock, including Tom. Tom was still standing at the plate, his eyes tightly shut, waiting for the call of strike, when he heard a familiar voice yell out over the crowd from the direction of third base.

"Run, Tom, run for first base. You hit the ball."

Tom ran down the baseline for dear life, arriving safe on first just before Corey's teammates had recovered their composure and the ball and had gotten it to first.

The next batter up, the Tigers' pride and joy at the plate, did what no one had ever seen done before. He pounded the ball out straight to center field. But it didn't go over the fence for a clean home run; it hit a rock out in center field, bounced high, and went over the fence. The outfielders on Corey's team ran for the fence and, in a Keystone Cops panic, ate precious time in boosting one of their players over the fence to retrieve the ball.

With his teammates yelling at him across the field, Tom headed around the bases, with the slugger hot on his tail. Tom had pulled up lame in his unfamiliar dash for first base, though, and it was an increasingly painful ordeal to hobble around the infield bases. His movement became slower and slower, his hobble more pronounced, the pressing slugger more and more angry and vocally threatening, as Tom approached third base.

I saw Corey looking out to the field beyond the fence, where his teammate was having trouble locating the ball in the thick underbrush, and I could see the struggle going on within my boy from the changing expressions on his face. He was in position to catch the ball if it could reach him in time and tag Tom or the slugger out so that his team could either win or tie the game. But I could see how conflicted he was—just how much he wanted his best friend, Tom, to get to home, if only this one time in his Little League career.

Tom stumbled past him at third, and the slugger pulled up there, waiting for Tom to get out in front of him. But Tom collapsed to the ground, exhausted and his right leg now useless, fifteen feet beyond third. He struggled on, though, pulling his body along with his now-bleeding elbows, determined to do all he could to make home.

I saw Corey's head swiveling back and forth, following the progress of the hunt for the ball out beyond center field and monitoring Tom's progress in the stretch of dirt between third and home.

And then I could see that Corey made a decision. My heart swelled and there was a roar of approval—even from the parents of Corey's teammates around me, I was thrilled to note—as I saw him dash out from third, lift up Tom in his arms, and drag him home.

They never did find the ball out there in the brush beyond the center field fence, and I'm probably the only one who knows why—who knows that it was something that had to be for both Corey and Tom to be winners that day.

Clyde Saves Christmas

Olivia Stowe

(From *Spirit of Christmas*)

Christine and Clyde loved Anne and Jim Randall's house. It spread out on many levels and had all sorts of interesting rooms filled with a lifetime of treasures—although Jim called it Oriental junk—from years of residence in East Asia and the Middle East.

Christine was partial to the tall carved wooden pillar that had come off a Thai temple and that Jim referred to as his Thai toothpick. Whenever the Randalls weren't looking, Christine stretched up on this pillar and pretended to sharpen her front claws on its rough wood, claws that she could only pretend to sharpen, because the Randalls had had hers removed when she was just a kitten. But she was most enticed by the large pottery wine jars the Randalls had brought back from the Middle East and kept in their den. Christine had graduated from one cool, dark pot to the next larger one as she grew from a kitten into a refined middle-aged lady. She could spend most of a day curled up inside whatever pot she currently fit through the top, dreaming of goldfish swirling around in a pond.

For his part, to Clyde, who was old enough to no longer be labeled as middle aged, the most intriguing treasures in the Randalls' collection were the two rattan elephant side tables. The rattan sides of the tables were just right for sharpening the front claws he didn't have either. And the elephants' wooden tusks were perfect for scratching the itches Clyde couldn't get to with his hind claws, which he still had. Clyde was just as attracted to the big, cool earthenware pots as Christine was, but he rarely jumped in one, because he had found that his arthritis prevented him from jumping out of even the largest pot opening on his own anymore.

Christmas morning found Christine and Clyde in seventh heaven, staring down the twinkling colored lights, batting at low-slung balls on the tree, and cavorting around the ribbons and wrapping paper Anne and Jim had strewn around on the floor of the den as they opened their presents and oohed and awed over the knickknacks friends and family assumed they still were collecting for their overstuffed house.

Christine looked up at the strange sound coming from Anne and the tearing up of her mistress's eyes as Anne held up a delicate black necklace. Christine sniffed at it, discerning that it was made out of human hair, which she'd never known to compose any of those other fascinating, shiny things Anne wore around her neck and wrists and on her ears. Just human hair. That must be why Anne was so sad about the present, Christine reasoned. It wasn't shiny; it was just human hair—very old human hair at that. If she'd really been able to understand those noises humans made, of course, Christine would have known that the present had been a belatedly delivered legacy from Anne's Aunt Suzie, who had died two months earlier, and who had asked that Anne receive this family heirloom made of Anne's great-grandmother's hair at Christmas time with the message that Aunt Suzie knew Anne would preserve and cherish it—and, in her own time, pass it on—as no one else in the family would.

But to Christine, the present had just made Anne sad—just as the bright gold cuff links Jim had just opened had made him laugh. Christine didn't need to translate the human noises to know why Jim was amused with this present. Ever since the Randalls and their Siamese cats had flown over the ocean from that exotic, tropical place Christine and Clyde had been born, Jim refused to wear anything that would require such shiny fasteners at his wrists. Christine knew Jim had had enough of that life, and she was just as happy that he spent most of his days now in the house, providing lap and extra strokes. But she'd also heard him bemoan not being able to wear half of his shirts because, for some unknown reason, they only worked when put together with those shiny gold things.

The shiny wrist fasteners frightened Christine somewhat. Did this mean Jim was going to be gone from the house more now? Was he going back to his old life? Would she be cooped up in that jostling cage in the belly of a big silver bird again? Christine hadn't liked that at all. And she wished she could do something now to keep that from happening.

The Randalls moved to the breakfast room, leaving Christine and Clyde to roll around in the stray wrappings until Clyde got bored and Christine got tired.

Later in the day, Christine awoke to the sound of Anne frantically searching around in the den for something. Christine emerged from her pot and tried to help Anne look, although she had no idea what Anne was looking for and Anne seemed to become even more frantic, with Christine rubbing against her leg as she searched around the room. Earlier in the afternoon, Jim had cleared the wrapping paper out. He had marched off with it wadded up in his arms and was now burning it in the fireplace in the living room.

Anne walked quickly to the living room, with Christine right behind her, and started to make those quick, insistent noises that humans seemed to need to make to communicate with each other. Jim made the noises back at her, and they both looked toward the fireplace with the saddest expressions on their faces that Christine had ever seen the two make.

For the rest of the afternoon, Anne wandered listlessly around the house with tears in her eyes and Jim seemed to have disappeared beyond that door in the breakfast room that led to a cold room filled with a couple of big metal cans. At last, Anne settled in an armchair in the den and stared at the Christmas tree, not really seeing it because of the tears that kept building up in her eyes. Christine hopped onto Anne's lap and let Anne stroke her. Christine knew that was the best medicine for whatever strange sickness Anne had.

Christine was the first one to hear the noise—a resonating, forlorn mewing that came from over by the Christmas tree. She knew instantly what the problem was, but it took Anne several minutes to even hear the noise, let alone to take any action. Christine hopped off Anne's lap an instant before Anne realized where the noise was coming from and what it meant. Christine beat her mistress to her current favorite earthenware pot in time to see Clyde's muzzle appear briefly at the neck of the pot and then disappear as he slid back down to the bottom.

Clyde was stuck in Christine's pot. Oh, no, Christine thought. Now the jig was up. Anne and Jim would really be sad now.

Anne reached over and turned the pot on its side so that Clyde could scamper out of his prison. As she did so, the lights of the tree glittered off something in the pot. She reached in with her hand and pulled out several ribbons and a bow— and Jim's new cuff links and Aunt Suzie's hair necklace.

Christine tried to tell her mistress that she was sorry, that she had tried to take the sadness away that the necklace brought to Anne earlier and to the danger of Jim having to go back to his old life, but, to her great surprise and disgust, Anne was laughing and squealing and hugging both Christine and Clyde and running off toward that door in the breakfast room in search of Jim, Clyde in full dash behind her.

Humans, Christine thought. They were so unpredictable and frustrating. She briefly sat and groomed herself for a few minutes, and then she picked up the ribbons and bow that Anne had left behind and retreated with them to her pot to dream of goldfish twirling around in a pond.

POETRY

No Longer in the Race

Lauvonda Lynn M. Young

I was a speeding train, running through
        life, married at eighteen, freshly
graduated high school, worked for
        necessities, fought glass ceiling
with some success, didn't ask for much

Tried to create babies, adopted instead,
        feverishly shaped a June Clever
family in tiny white house, minus picket
        fence, my son blossomed
beautifully, now he runs on his own

After staring point blank at my life
        swiftly winding down, I stopped
dancing to the tunes created by others,
        my fancy pen I took up, to tell my
narrative, never dreaming of profit

Old dreams, dressed in new apparel
        delivered new memories, to my
front door, nine to five disappeared, life
        is magnificent, I like its rhyme,
still no utopia, but everything's fine

Love Unconditional

Lauvonda Lynn M. Young

Come to me, beloved
    talk to me with your
    eyes, in language we
alone understand, provide
    assurance of your
devotedness, by planting
    memories, so I'll
have blooms, long after
    you're gone, there
are things I will forget, but
    not you, my precious
feline, Shadow Dancer . . . .

Sea Door

Stanley A. Galloway

(On a theme by Kazim Ali. Third prize, Judah, Sarah, Grace,
and Tom Memorial, Poetry Society of Virginia, 2015)

the sea laps like a hand rap
on the door of my soul.
at six years old I did not know
how to answer—I could only hear
that water-muffled call
with paralyzed response.

intuition told me something called
                    beneath the surface
where keels and barnacles are wed
                    amid the lulling lurch
                        of fumbling lovers.

my soul is moored lightly tonight,
seeing the sun descend into Cyprian water
the way that I will from the back balcony
when I understand the mechanism of the latch.

then I, too, can go,
learning
            to read the refracted slate of constellations
            to hear the echo of the stars pulse
            to understand the dancing compass
            intersects two worlds and has
            forgotten which is real,
            to know that needle points the way.

Ringtone

Stanley A. Galloway

(First honorable mention, Raymond Levi Haislip Memorial,
Poetry Society of Virginia, 2015)

Two women washing clothes
beside the creek
outside Nairobi,
chatted with each other
while their bodies swayed
in scrubbing motions.

Colorful print blouses
held their braless bosoms half in check,
exposing chocolate skin in shadowed flashes.

A day from any recent century it seemed
until I heard a cell phone ring
and one set down the shirt she'd soaked
and answered,
   laughing briefly,
   talking quickly,
   raising up her eyes
   to search the hillside opposite.

A minute later she began to wave
at someone half-grown walking on the ridge,
an infant bundled on her back.
"Mama" she chimed,
a ringtone
from the dawn of life.

My Lass in County Kerry

Stanley A. Galloway

(Second honorable mention, Come Out Swinging Prize, Poetry
Society of Virginia, 2015)

The rain is cold and I feel old
I've more than I can carry
The only thing that makes me sing
Is my lass in County Kerry

She's a hungry lass of the working class
And I'm a poor man, too
But I can plumb, so the day will come
When I bid Dundalk adieu

The rain is cold and I feel old
I've more than I can carry
The only thing that makes me sing
Is my lass in County Kerry

So I'll ply my trade in a grand parade
Of jobs from north to south
And I'll haul my trunks to the Skellig monks
To put kisses on her mouth

The rain is cold and I feel old
I've more than I can carry
The only thing that makes me sing
Is my lass in County Kerry

And we can eat by the burning peat
In a little stone cottage by the sea
The wind and the rain won't be much pain
With my Kerry lass by me

The rain is cold and I feel old
And I've more than I can carry

The only thing that makes me sing
Is my lass in County Kerry

For Plato and My Mother

David Black

(Third place poetry, Virginia Writers Club Summer Shorts, 2015)

Railing against literacy, the old Greek
said it would destroy a man's memory
by letting him forget what he could write down.
I find myself reliving the truth of it,
searching for a scrap of paper and a pen,
muttering, "Now let me write this down
so I won't forget it," all the time meaning
"Let me write this down so I **can** forget it."
Putting your name and birth and death
on a tombstone and then walking away.

Spring Plowing

David Black

(First place poetry, *Skyline* spring contest, 2015)

There's a *before* and *after* in this story,
and maybe several more. I don't know it all.

For me it began in the garden
one spring day when I was ten.

The Farmall had reached mid-field
when it hung up—reared like a startled horse

and spun its back wheels—listed to the right,
the plowed side, as that tire dug in deep.

Dad cut the engine, stopped, reversed;
lifted the plow with the PTO;

and there it was: a jagged break
where the front end of the share used to be.

We dug. Swearing over two bent crowbars
and a broken shovel till we got a chain around it

and hauled it out with the tractor.
As big as a tombstone and thicker,

but unmarked except where the chain had dug in
and a gouge on one edge from the plow.

Not a tombstone, though, nor a pedestal
for a long-buried statue, nor a paving stone

in an ancient road which once led somewhere.
Just a rock, as all this soil once had been.

And as it dried and warmed in the April sun,

changed to the less alien tan

of my own hands and face, I thought,
as I do again, that the day is coming

when I, too, will go underground
and become what this stone is trying to be.

Earth is easy to get lost in:
We slip into that unseen shade

for a tranquil while, and then comes the time
when it all starts over, when we emerge again,

when we'll drift across the earth
in the slightest breeze and try to remember

back to that time, long seasons ago,
when whatever we were had a name.

Chinese Food in Florence, Italy

Linda Levokove
(First place poetry, Blue Ridge Writers Chapter VWC, 2015)

The gusty night wind awakens me.
At the window I look at the rows
of ornate black iron street lamps
casting a golden glow on the Arno.

Earlier, strolling on the Bridge of Sighs
we argued . . . you flapping your hands,
me shouting.

Back in our tiny room we ate Chinese food
and made love for a long time—until
shadows crept up the worn frescoed walls.

Afterward, we slept like the curled noodles
that had fallen on the chipped terrazzo floor.

I knew this wasn't love forever . . . just for now,
and like Chinese food, I knew we would soon
be hungry again.

A Spring Romance

Linda Levokove

We're ghosts enchanted with transparency,
visible yet illusive as the light in our eyes

as the ever wavering sea constantly renews
even as we wait impatiently for darkness

to capture the last likeness before it's sheered
by the ripples of water, baffled and blurred.

We're nothing more than reflections we see,
no less than the shine we cast on one another,

and the breeze-bent Jonquils, fresh and green,
stroked by the sunlight on this dazzling day . . .

so stay, until I can't hear the wind in the willows,
the cicadas silenced, and flitting butterflies stilled—

stay, till white stars disappear and moonlight dims,
and the spring's fresh silver rain ceases to fall.

Seed

Erin Newton Wells
(Second place poetry, Blue Ridge Writers Chapter VWC, 2015)

Generations spiral from trees,
maple wings paper thin.
So many miss the mark. They land
and waste whole drifts
in my hair, my pockets, my hands.
I do them no good.
I am no earth to birth these seeds.

They want to send white roots down,
slim searching strands
in dark soil, so new leaves appear.
They want to continue.
And I am foreign, barren
to this unborn forest.
It needs another fertile ground.

But let the idea of them come
sailing like maple seeds,
a light cotyledon of thought
borne to my mind,
let it settle as word and sprout,
I will make infants
more numerous than all their young.

A Late Spring

Erin Newton Wells

(Second place poetry, *Skyline* spring contest, 2015)

Fuchsia shouts from a million mouths,
then unexpected coral,
then lavish white is poured
with lipstick red
all at once and all the more
impatient to begin,
all of it out of sequence now.

Spring this year is over the top,
flamboyant with warmth
switched on after delay
when winter would not go
and snow after snow stayed
too long, too cold,
and every urge to grow stopped.

Azalea explodes. Then tulip
in multitude, crocus,
hyacinth, daffodil make one blast
from thawed ground.
The root, the bulb, the corm at last
shake off what held
in an everlasting grip.

Forsythia, the redbud, the pear,
splatters of dogwood
shoot in brilliance, color renewed,
startling rockets
against an air charged with stunned blue,
a shocking load
it almost cannot bear.

Exposed

Erin Newton Wells

(Third place poetry, Fralin Museum of Art Writers' Eye
contest, 2013; written on image by Emilie Charmy, "Self-
Portrait in an Open Dressing Gown," which can be viewed at
http://www.the-athenaeum.org/art/detail.php?ID=163234)

It all starts to slide, first the silk wrapper
from the shoulders. A hand drops the sash,
autobiography still smoldering
on the startled breast. After the blood rebels
who can remember the parables?

An eye droops. The mouth questions. The light
begins to cool on a moonscape of ash.

Did you give me this gown of quiet silver,
slip me into its silence, surround me
with the slow, spun turnings of your mind?

Was it another in the crumbled sun
of Corsica, eyes mirroring water
filled with flame, words of no absolute shade,
hands of fallen feathers burned to cinder?

Imagine War

Sigrid Mirabella
(Third place poetry, Blue Ridge Chapter VWC, 2015)

I imagine you sleeping, cuddled with your rifle,
the way they taught you to treat it as a lover
—hold tight, keep close, treat with honor.

I see you with a pillow of cold sand
molded beneath your unrisen head
before alarms wake you to another burning day.

I think about you blasting rap music
with freedom lyrics of your invention
—*For thee I sing, bring home the bling-bling.*

I sense you might want to go to college, become
a doctor, undo damage you've seen, taken part
in, bandage wounds, cleanup the blood.

I create a name for you, wonder your age,
presume you fantasize about whom you'll marry,
guess how many children might be conceived.

I decide you probably have brothers, perhaps one
not born yet, but you worry about him, already
wanting to fill a big brother's shoes.

I hear your sisters crying, your parents
denying any possibility of you lost in conflict
or swaddled in dark plastic, folded flag at their door.

I watch you on TV broadcasts, burdened back,
eyes pinched sideways searching for suiciders
awaiting virgins, dead already, planning your death.

I pray for you, Godless I at ease, concerned about
you from my comfortable couch, watching war
manipulated by producer, director, angle of camera.

Grass Vengeance

Sigrid Mirabella

All night while I sleep
the lawn grows
creeps over worms
roots ensnare stones

green the color
of abundance gone wild
Daybreak stimulates
rampaging lengths

Two inches rise to four
blades thicken
hideouts for ticks
waiting for hosts

A flattened snake-trail
above tunneled moles
suggests time to mow
fourth time this week

I wake-up cut lawn
go off to my job
Later back home pull-start
my overwhelmed mower

cut grass until the sun drops
before loss of vision
stops all today's work
though not for tomorrow

I'm mowed-over
so much needs cutting still
Tonight I know the grass
will grow while I sleep

So I don't pray anymore for love to find me
only beg no more rain for the time being

Lesson from a Narcissus

Elizabeth Doyle Solomon

(Third place poetry, *Skyline* spring contest, 2015)

Narcissus blooms his fragrant whites
in my April garden today;
I know better than to ask him
why all winter in the dark he lay.

It must give him great joy to rise
releasing this petaled perfume;
what a gift is his blossoming,
not a day too late or too soon.

Beautiful youth who refused all love,
even from exquisite Echo;
he fell in love with his image,
died for conceit. Is it not so?

In a glass vase he speaks no words,
but his self-love is a lesson.
Let beauty own no vanity,
nor praise its own possession.

(Narcissus: In Greek mythology, a beautiful youth who refused
all love, even that of Echo. He fell in love with his own image
in a pool, and pining away, died for love of himself.
Narcissus poeticus: Poet's narcissus has very fragrant, creamy-
white flowers with an orange-red center.)

Death of the Second Frontier:
Ode to America from Civil War to Moon Landing

Gary D. Kessler

Well, Grandmother told us how it would be.
"The first day in a hospital will be the end for me."
The death of the second American frontier—that's tough,
because I didn't ask or listen to her enough.

Born in the echo of the last shot smother
Of the war remembered as
Brother against brother.

Leveled by the Spanish flu plague,
"Your choices are to bury your husband
or comfort two children on their last leg."

Leaving the vanished lap of the best
to homestead in the Rockies,
last hurrah of the truly wild, wild West.

Before, living in a modernizing world still small,
with advent of cars, electricity, department stores,
Henry F. Thomas E, and J.C. Penny friends she did call.

Years later, sitting in gallery of U.S. Senate Chamber.
Hearing her whisper, "I should have let the foot wound fester,"
As old friend Edwin Johnston parroted Joseph McCarthy's bluster.

Seen, known, experienced so much of the past,
gathering a wealth of rich memory
when the world wasn't as crowded and didn't whirl as fast.

Wise enough when moon landing commentator spun
declaration of "the end of the frontier,"
she murmured, "No, just the beginning of a new one."

But on that day, in the wake of her only hospital stay
The death to me of the second American frontier way,
Because I didn't ask enough, listen enough before that
day.

Alas, now only a momentous "was there" era of a
woman's fading memory,
that someday soon will die too with me.

April Mantis

Leonard Tuchyner

Tiny insect brown and modest,
sitting so still on her finger,
cocking your clever little head.
Are you harmless or rather coy?

Arctic-March is just a fortnight past.
Yet here you are, a pinky-nail's width.
I know you're not a peaceful vegan.
Did you dine on your brothers and kind?

How did you know it would be safe
to rest serene on my wife's hand
which like a mantis, can be lethal.
One twitch of thumb could crush you to mush.

How did you know she would gently
set you on a redbud limb's bark
and bless you for a long-lived life,
honoring skillful predation?

If wise and lucky in your ways,
you will grow longer than that kind hand,
fast enough to capture lizards,
and breed a brood of some hundreds,
before you die a hero's death,
face demise by nasty lover,
or pass away in Winter's breath.

I welcome you to my garden.

PROSE NONFICTION

Reflections on Running for Congress

Jack Trammell

Running for Congress is not like speed dating and flying to Vegas to get married—it's more like holding a live hornet's nest in your hands and shaking it up and telling yourself that everything will work out okay in the next thirty seconds. One minute later, you are forced to repeat the process.

I never thought that I would become the person that everyone was interested in—just as I never thought in a million years that Eric Cantor would lose in the Republican primary. But life, to paraphrase Ian Malcolm, will not just find a way, it will then shock your hand when you least expect it to remind you that it finds a way.

That night of the primary, I was giving a stump speech as the recently announced "sacrificial lamb" to a meeting of Democrats in my home, Louisa County. The library meeting room had maybe a dozen people total in attendance. As I talked about public-private transportation financing reform with great enthusiasm, I noticed that many people were not looking at me—they were sneaking furtive glances at their smart phones and tablets. Before I could be offended, someone blurted out:

"Brat is actually winning! Our strategy to get Democrats out to vote for him is working!"

A rippling murmur spread around the room, and the chair politely rapped the table and reminded everyone that a guest speaker was present.

"Let's give Jack the respect he deserves as the newly announced Democratic candidate," she said.

"He's ahead by three thousand votes!" someone else said.

"Brat is actually winning."

"Channel 6 just called the election for Brat!"

The room erupted. Even if you, dear reader, don't follow Virginia politics, you still may remember this night. Perhaps it's not like 9/11, or when Kennedy was shot, but this was the most dramatic political shot heard round the world in quite some time. I now think of it as a second landing of a man on the moon.

I was still standing at the podium, ready to talk about the new bay tunnel, which was being constructed of concrete, rather than steel, and represented a massive waste of taxpayer dollars, and a safety risk. I decided to step outside and catch some fresh air, and as I did, a normal-strength signal returned to my iPhone. I have never seen anything like what happened next.

First, the device made some strange sounds, in spite of being muted. Secondly, the missed calls message came up on the screen and revealed dozens of calls (soon to be hundreds) that had come through in the last few minutes. There were an equal number of new texts, and hundreds of new, unknown e-mails. Then, before I could even process the information, the phone began ringing (vibrating actually) with a call from an unknown number. In my stunned state, I picked up:

"Jack! Where are you?"

"In a parking lot beside the library. Who is this?"

"It's [redacted]. Don't talk to anyone! Do you understand? I don't care if President Obama himself calls, do not answer!"

"What?"

"Now listen to me closely. How many people know where you are?"

I admit. I was flustered. I love James Bond movies, but I had never imagined myself living in one. I had barely begun to process the primary upset. The iPhone was so hot that I could barely hold it in my hand. People were coming out of the library, apparently having finally recognized the amazing position I was in, as well as the startling moment in political history, and they were reaching their hands out to me—to what? Congratulate me? Lay hands on me? Or what—ask for a job already?

"No one really knows where I am. Maybe my wife, Audrie, but she's with her kids . . ."

"Then, listen closely. I want you to turn your phone off, and drive to the [redacted] in the West End, and it's very important that you talk to no one. . . . No speeding tickets or bathroom stops! Do you understand?"

While he was talking to me, messages were appearing on the periphery of my screen—Fox News, MSNBC, BBC—wait, MSNBC? Rachel Madow! I always wanted to be on Rachel's show. NBC, CBS, ABC—they could wait. CNN, though, shouldn't I call them back? Al Jazeera, Reuters, the *Washington Post*. The *Post*? Maybe I could *finally* get them to run that exposé on P3 (public-private partnerships) transportation scandals that I had been pushing them about for weeks.

People were pulling at me and all talking over each other—at me and through me—and I realized that the phone conversation had ended, but I couldn't remember how. The iPhone was still positively scorching in my hand. It continued ringing constantly and beeping like a broken smoke detector. I glanced at my e-mail—over six hundred. Text messages, over one hundred. Missed calls, over one hundred. How did these people get my cell phone number? (I later found out there are all kinds of things about me on the Internet, including my cell phone number . . .)

"I have to go," I said quietly, trying to nod my head, smile, and be polite.

"But we already called some people who are coming to interview you!"

Panic. I was told in no uncertain terms to talk to no one. Not even Rachel Madow. I didn't want my campaign to begin and end in the parking lot at the library in Louisa.

"I really have to go. Thank you again for the food and asking me to come and speak."

Into the 2010 blue Ford Ranger. Out of the parking lot, carefully, as people continued to follow me. (Has anyone famous ever driven an old Ford Ranger?) Palm fronds on the pavement? On to Route 33. I knew that I had to call Audrie.

"Jack, I've been trying to call you. Can you believe this? You're all over the news! They're using a picture of you from the college! This is unreal! Every channel I turn on is talking about you and the other guy."

She had taken to her early campaign training. She wasn't calling my opponent by his name. Part of me that wasn't in shock was briefly impressed. Good Audrie!

"I have to go to a hotel. I'll call you after I'm settled there."

"What? Where? Hey, Mary and I are coming to see you. Where are you? Where are you going? Hey, I need to know what is going on—"

"I will call you in a little bit."

I didn't dare turn on the radio. My iPhone was already bleeding the news to me moment by moment, through every App installed. The phone rang again, and now angry at the hijacking of my life, I rebelled and started to answer. As I drove the next forty minutes, I talked to [redacted], a governor and famous former presidential almost; [redacted], a famous Hollywood action movie director and political junkie; and my old friend and campaign manager, who was more freaked out than me.

When I arrived at the hotel, a group of young party people dressed in business formal swept into the lobby and looked me over. I think I had on flip-flops, khaki shorts, and a homemade "I back Jack!" T-shirt. This outfit was okay, really, for a talk at the library in Louisa before I was famous. But it now evidently was cause for me to have to produce a photo ID to prove who I really was.

"I'll start looking at wardrobe," the blonde said, with a plastic smile that I appreciated given the circumstances, although clearly she viewed me as a challenge already.

Behind her, another young woman was on the phone, completely ignoring me.

"Well, you tell Rachel that she will just have to wait like everyone else. He's NOT available now."

The eldest of the group smiled and shook my hand; he seemed calm and that certainly drew me in like a magnet.

"Jack, we've reserved the business suite on the Penthouse Level where we have started to set up a temporary command center for your campaign. I know this must be a little overwhelming, but don't worry, we'll get it all under control. We need all your passwords and online IDs as soon as you can put those together for me, from Facebook to finance. Really, we'll have to get to work on that ASAP." He turned to another underling. "Get the fund-raising page up immediately!" Back to me, "Jack, do you have all that information with you?"

"I need to let Audrie know where I am."

"Oh, don't worry! We've been in contact with her. We're guiding her in, but we've got some work to do first. Come on!"

I followed them into the elevator. They were all on their phones yelling, questioning, explaining—some of them were on two phones at the same time, one at each ear.

The command center consisted of a series of laptops on a table that normally held trays of breakfast items. Each laptop had a person on a stool parked at it, and each one had a specific task.

"Jack, Facebook login and password?"

"Jack, we need a picture of you, do you have any with you?"

"Jack, I need you to approve this statement for the AP wire."

A friend of a party staff person, clearly drunk, had followed the party into the hotel and was now sitting beside me. We both were watching me on TV, and then laughing about it. She put her hand on my knee.

"This is much more exciting than the earlier event tonight," she said. "I'm glad they didn't let me drive myself home!" She had on a revealing sequin dress, and here I was, completely outfitted like a bad cowboy. It didn't seem to bother her. She was devouring a messy cheeseburger.

"You want a bite?"

"[Redacted]," I said.

Audrie appeared as if by magic, and the event then took on a party-like atmosphere as she suggested ordering pizza and going out for beer. The party people, however, continued hacking away on their laptops. That didn't stop Audrie, who set up her own media station to order pizza and call friends.

"He's up to $50,000," someone called out. "I've never seen someone do $50,000 in the first two hours. Never . . ."

"Keep that Web site up!"

That night taught me several things that I will never forget. First and foremost, one should never assume that they know what will happen next. The unimaginable can and does happen; it restored my faith in the great, wide unknown.

Second of all, it taught me that politics has its own set of rules that are not governed by physical laws or the media:

"Jack, the governor is on the line—he wants to talk to you."

Thirdly, it taught me that life is short, and you should take chances to do something special. You may go down in flames, but you may also make a difference. You'll never know unless you try.

"Jack, you look like you need a beer. Hey, someone! Get him a beer!"

"I like IPA," I said quietly.

"Get him an IPA!"

Lastly, I have to say that it's good to be king. Even if it's only for a few hours of one night. It is good.

The Time Capsule

Susan M. Lanterman

It's a recurring dream. I am in the second story of my grandparents' Victorian cottage. I have pushed against a wall, and it mysteriously opens into a room filled with trunks, armoires, and antique furniture. The scene is reminiscent of *Great Expectations*, where time stands still under a layer of dust and cobwebs. My eyes glaze over at the endless objects to discover. I am ecstatic.

When I was a child, my grandparents purchased an ominous-looking, three-story "cottage" on the Connecticut shore for summer vacations. Behind its mahogany door and cedar shakes, the rooms were fully furnished with relics from the late 1800s—when it was last inhabited. It appeared as if the previous owners had simply vanished, taking nothing with them. My grandparents were minimalists and unimpressed by the mildewed contents. "Junka, junka, junka," grandma would chant in her Italian accent as she entered a room with too many accouterments. The pump organ, Philco radio, and marble-topped tables were of little value to her. She gave away chamber pots and other antiques to anyone who visited, as if they were door prizes.

The centerpiece of the kitchen was a large gas stove that provided heat in the damp, misty mornings. We gathered like chicks around the old mother hen. Across from it squatted another modern marvel my grandmother fondly referred to as the "ice box." Inside there was limited space to store items you hoped wouldn't freeze and a freezer the size of a Jack-in-the-Box that froze everything into one block of ice. There was a roomy pantry filled with Depression glass, mismatched china, and what was once considered new-fangled gadgets: an oscillating fan with brass blades that resembled a boat propeller, a glass-topped coffee percolator, and one of the first electric toasters designed to brown one side of your bread at a time. All of which couldn't be plugged in without sparks flying.

The enormous dining table nearly consumed the room but allowed for a brood of twelve to sit comfortably under the watchful eye Cuckoo clock.

Upstairs were bedrooms with saddleback mattresses, feather pillows, and an array of patchwork quilts—all smelling like the bottom of a gerbil cage. The only bathroom was outfitted with a claw foot tub and a sink with separate hot and cold taps so you would alternate scalding or freezing your hands when washing.

As a kid growing up in a four-room flat in the city, visiting the cottage was like a trip to the Haunted Mansion at Disneyland. On weekends my parents packed up the car and caravanned with several other families to our personal "fun house" by the sea. My older sister (with the overactive imagination) would tell tales of our "creepy attic" to any perspective scaredy-cat child in tow. The attic was the only room my father didn't disturb in his efforts to modernize the place. It was locked with a skeleton key, to ensure its dusty contents would remain intact. We had scoured every inch of all the other musty rooms, scrutinizing the contents of each drawer and closet. The prospect of hidden treasure lured us from the inhabited into the forbidden.

After locating the key to the attic door, we would tiptoe up its winding stairs, reminding our visitors not to awaken the spirits that resided above. As my sister slowly opened squeaky doors and drawers, she would spin tales about the contents found within. Scissors and what looked like a ball of hair—cut in grief by the widow of a sailor lost at sea. A brass ring, that belonged to a pirate who was known to pace the floors looking for it.

The attic provided the perfect backdrop for spooky stories. Windows mysteriously opened, allowing bats to nest in the eves and spiders to connect the shabby furnishings with finely spun cobwebs that entangled the unsuspected. Our tours were reserved for daylight hours and only for a short time, as our guests would never linger. At night we would lie shoulder to shoulder on the damp bed, while ocean winds whistled through the rickety walls overhead, further embellishing our yarns with creaks and moans.

Sadly, my parents sold the cottage when I was a teenager. It was offered "lock, stock, and barrel" just as it was when it was purchased. My parents, like my grandparents, also thought the interiors were filled with historic hodge-podge that were simply old fashioned and worthless. Before the sale I boxed up sentimental items—a framed Maxwell Parrish print, a few Blue Willow dishes, the toaster, one remaining chamber pot—things I still have. At the time, I wondered if these were just childish attachments.

But much to my family's dismay I have continued to rescue cast-off heirlooms, cramming them into corners and perching them on bookshelves—my grandfather's Kodak box camera, my father-in-law's Royal typewriter, my great-cousin's treadle sewing machine. When you begin hording unwanted items, you find things left in a box at your door like a stray kitten.

I've worried that the pendulum will swing and all my precious treasures will be cast off by my offspring someday. For now, they reside in the Victorian home my husband and I purchased. Built in 1890, it had barely been brought into the twentieth century. While many would-be inhabitants before us were frightened away, we saw through the grime and shabby interior. As I walked the rooms, I ran my hand along the wavy walls, hoping for some movement—a sliding panel, a hidden door. I searched the nooks and crannies but there were no surprises. My dream would remain dormant.

Then one day while my kids were helping remove some plaster walls, they called out excitedly, "We finally found a treasure!" Behind the oak mantle was a small trove of memorabilia—a handmade business card from the man who built the piece, an exam book from the University of Virginia, a photo of a girl standing in front of our house tucked within an accompanying letter, all dating back to the house's origin. As we gathered around the dining room table and inspected our little time capsule, my son read the text aloud while my daughter began to transcribe the letter, straining to read the faded ink on the sepia colored paper. I was ecstatic.

Crossing the Street: Connecting through Dream Work

Phyllis Koch-Sheras, PhD

I am with my adolescent daughter in a strange city at night. Suddenly, she runs across a busy street into the traffic. I'm scared and scream at her. Then we get in my car and attempt to drive out of the city. We get lost. I come to two barricades and a one-way street going the wrong way. I'm frustrated but confident we will find a way out eventually . . .

I say to myself, "This is a dream" (which it is) and that I can change it (which I do). As I focus on the key feelings and aspects of the dream, I see the three blockades I encounter as the "three poisons" in the Tibetan Buddhist tradition I am studying while on retreat that week: ignorance, aversion, and attachment. The night I turned the wrong way recently down the 250 East bypass in Charlottesville comes rushing back to me. I start shaking and then say again, "This is a dream." I also recall other times in my life when I ended up in dangerous situations (a fire in our house, accidents while skiing, driving a car, and a motorcycle). I keep saying, "This is a dream," and feel the anxiety and aversion begin to dissipate.

I recognize my attachment to my daughter and my difficulty letting go of her as a child and seeing her as a competent adult, which she definitely is now as a mother of her own daughter. I imagine watching her cross the street (to adulthood) and feel at peace, saying, "it's OK," rather than screaming after her to be careful. I can trust her now to leave the nest and go on to create her own life separate from me. I see that I am also crossing my own barriers, learning to trust myself to be careful and mindful as I grow into the latter part of my life, and forgiving myself for the mistakes of the past. The blockages are my path to healing and enlightenment, not something to avoid or ignore. They are "dream helpers," there to alert me and expand my awareness for my own well-being and for the benefit of others. I feel a wave of gratitude for my family and my teachers, thankful that we are surviving and thriving in the face of all the obstacles out there in the world.

I return from the retreat and call our daughter and tell her about the dream. She is just getting home from work, playing with her daughter and their dog as she begins to prepare dinner for the family. She tells me about their financial pressures as her husband prepares to have his wisdom teeth extracted. I tell her how proud of her I am and how much I trust her to handle it all. I also tell her we will let the tooth fairy (our bank!) know to leave something for those teeth. We are able to lighten up about it all and end up laughing as her husband comes home from work and joins in the fun.

Doing dream work has been a part of my emotional, professional, and spiritual life for over forty years. It has helped me become aware of the deeper issues in my life and to expand my consciousness and acceptance of both the positive and negative parts of myself and others and to help other people do the same for themselves. That, for me, is the real value of dream work, not just to understand the meaning of a dream or to resolve current circumstances, but also to make a deep connection within myself and with others. Dreams are not only *about* relationships; they can actually change and create relationships. This happens by clearing the negative blocks within you as they manifest in the dream content (like the distrustful part of me in the dream above) and by sharing the dream with others in your life, as I did with my daughter.

A simple method of working on dreams that I have developed involves translating the dream into "dream language" (Koch-Sheras and Lemley, 1998). It involves rephrasing the dream in a way that focuses on everything in the dream representing parts of yourself, created by you, the dreamer, who is the writer, producer, and actor of all the parts of your dream play or movie. This is based on the Jungian notion that all aspects of life exist in every human being, positive and negative alike. In this sense, we are not in the universe; the universe exists in us.

Dream Language is a present-tense language, so start by telling or writing down the dream in the present tense, as if it is happening now. That makes it come more alive for both you and the listener and may even help you remember more of the significant details of the dream. Next, add the phrase "I have me" to the beginning of each new sentence or phrase to emphasize that you are creating the dream rather than that it is just happening to you. Translating the dream in this way makes it clear that we are responsible for what happens to us, both in our waking life as well as in the dream stories we make up. Lastly, add the phrase "part of me" to all the nouns in the dream, enabling you to "own" each part of the dream as a part of yourself and your own perceptions or projections.

In my dream above, for example, "I have me be scared about the daughter part of me crossing the street part of me; I have me confront barriers part of me," and so on. Pay particular attention to your feelings in the dream, especially at the end of it, as they are a guide to your deeper consciousness. After you have translated the dream, give it a title, which helps give it even more focus. I gave the dream above the title "Crossing the Street," which helped me see that "it's OK" and "I'm OK" to take risks, move on with my life, and trust others I love to do the same.

The ultimate dream work, according to the Tibetan Buddhist Bon teacher, Tenzin Wangyal Rinpoche, and others is the state of lucid dreaming, that is, being aware that you are dreaming while you are dreaming. While lucid, the dreamer has choice and power and can control the mysteries of the unconscious mind in the moment. Becoming lucid is facilitated by saying, "This is a dream" in both waking and dreaming life, "realizing that waking life is actually the same as a dream . . . and that whatever we experience is due to the influence of karma" (T.W. Rinpoche, page 91). According to this philosophy, when lucidity in the dream state is fully developed, "we will also be preparing ourselves to attain liberation . . . after death" (page 17).

Whatever way you may experience your dreams, there are a multitude of gifts to be received from them. We spend nearly one-third of our life asleep, with a significant amount of that time in the dream state. Why waste it? This is valuable time that we can learn to remember, respect, and use to create connections for the benefit of ourselves and others. Learning the language of dreams, like any other new language, takes time to develop and master. I hope that sharing my dream and dream work techniques will motivate and help you to work on your own dreams. I leave you with this poem that I wrote based on a song from my childhood by Stephen Foster and the messages I got from "crossing the street" into the next phase of my life:

> Beautiful dreamer, Queen of my Song,
> I now know that you are me and I am you
> And that everything is a dream.
> Your music, sometimes dark and sometimes light,
> Is always a beautiful path to enlightenment.
> Beautiful dreamer, awake unto me;
> May I float on the wings of your precious melody
> From now until eternity.

References:

Tenzin Wangyal Rinpoche, *The Tibetan Yogas of Dream and Sleep*. N.Y.: Snow Lion Publications, 1998.

Phyllis Koch-Sheras and Amy Lemley, *The Dream Sourcebook* (Lincolnwood, Ill: NTC/Contemporary Publishing Group), 1998.

Bound

Brenda A. Morris

(First place nonfiction, Blue Ridge Writers Chapter VWC, 2015)

Insight comes when we least expect it. Standing in a cemetery with the owner of my small community's funeral home, looking at the gravestone of a couple who died forty years ago, and the grave of their son-in-law, who's been there twenty years, planning the stone for his still-living wife, I have an epiphany.

Frankie had drawn the plans for the new stone. He duly noted the names and dates to be put on it for the dead husband and for his still-living wife. We wander around, looking at other stones to compare sizes. I am annoyed that he needs to discuss other options with me. My mother's friend, now ninety-three, had told me she wanted a stone like her father and mother's stone. What's to discuss? Duplicate that stone with the new names and dates. But Frankie had his job to do, and part of it is to make sure the patron ordering the stone knows all the choices and is satisfied with the final decision. I don't really care about the stone. I only volunteered to talk to him because my mother's friend no longer travels, lives over 100 miles away, and is legally blind and hard of hearing. I was just being the conduit for making sure the stone was there when she needed it.

At sixty-three, I don't expect to need a stone any time soon. But I am a planner. I jokingly told Frankie that I'd be down in the near future to order my own stone. As soon as my husband decided if he wanted to be buried beside me, or in New York with his mother's family.

Frankie stopped and said he'd put up his own stone when his second wife died several months before. The tone changed. He said everyone had told him he shouldn't put up a double stone. "You might get married again," they said. "And then where would you be?"

"That's true," he said. "I might. But I know I want to be there next to my wife, regardless."

He looked at me, no longer the funeral director, but a man opening his soul to a friend. I was touched, honored, and uncomfortable, all at the same time. I muttered how sorry I was at his loss. And I was. Sorry that a good man had found his soul mate and lost her at the very moment they both should have been leaving the rat race of the work world and embarking on a journey of discovery and joy in the next phase of their lives. My recent retirement must have looked mockingly at him, because retirement for him would be lonely and empty without his wife beside him.

I was suddenly humbled. I realized the job I was doing, arranging a gravestone for my mother's friend, was so much more then the physical legwork of planning and ordering it. It was completing the journey she had made with her partner. Giving her, and the future generations, the assurance that her relationship was validated by bonding her and her husband together on a gravestone in the church yard forever. As Frankie had done with his wife and himself.

Thin Places

Erin Newton Wells
(Second place nonfiction, Blue Ridge Writers Chapter VWC, 2015)

The Irish describe certain locations as having immanence. Unusual things can happen there. A person entering the place might feel a heightened awareness, even a sense of luminosity. Everything seems more intense in a way not explained physically. People unused to thinking in this way might be uneasy when presented with the thought. They find what cannot be verified difficult to accept. The extraordinary is not allowed into their world. But this was not so in my family, where it was believed that anything might happen.

My Irish ancestry was drummed into me by a grandmother. She did not want me to forget her father, my great grandfather, who came from Ireland in the exit waves of the 1840s. He longed for the land he was forced to leave and kept it alive for her in stories and on a map of that green shape pinned to a wall of his room. She would speak of it to me with nearly a holy fervor, trying to hand me that legacy.

Because of this I grew up assuming my connection to the Irish mind. Later, as I began to study Early Irish literature and language, I found that the body of ideas and images actually did correlate closely with my own. The endless, intricate designs of Celtic braid and coils that represent the eternal seemed like ones drawn by my hand. The stark metaphors and voice of Early Irish poetry were as familiar as my own. It was all bathed in a numinous light of possibility and was a culture I felt I understood. Was I biased toward this by my grandmother? Had she planted it there? Or was it instinctive?

I remember the day I came across an account of Colm Cille, or Saint Columba, a sixth-century Irish priest. He sailed to a tiny, remote island off the western coast of Scotland to establish a monastic community. On it he felt a sense of the unearthly. It is described as a thin place. The sky, the very air, seemed so stretched to translucency that the extraordinary could more easily break through. The island is called Iona by some.

I have been in many thick places weighted down only with themselves. And I have been in other places that are thin, allowing something else to happen through them. I understood Iona, though surely this is not exclusively Irish. Those who are deeply attuned to the atmospheres around them will comprehend the idea.

But I shall go a step further and propose that not only places have thinness. Sometimes people do, too. For the past three years I found myself living in the proximity of a person who brought thinness among us. It was not the specific location where she happened to be. It was the person herself. Wherever she went, possibility went with her.

I did not recognize anything different at first. This thinning, shall we say, had not actually begun. A year into my association with her it all began to change. I knew something unusual was under way, and I soon discovered that other people realized it, too. They began to speak of it in the reserved and cautious manner of those not used to the inexplicable breaking into their known world. They responded more vigorously when I mentioned it in my voluble Irish way. They seemed relieved to learn they were not alone in picking up on the situation.

If I were the only one, call it the crazy Irish in me. But there were so many of these people who lived with fact, proof, and evidence, and they were thinking the same. They were not naturally given to mystical language. But they were beginning to speak it.

She came to us newly ordained as assistant clergy in our parish. All indications were she was good at her vocation, and she immediately gained our respect and affection. A little over a year later we saw that she was to be not good but great at what she was doing. This was after she was diagnosed with ALS.

The first sign was in the hands, which began to stiffen and curl, making it difficult for her to use them. She adapted. The announcement came to us in a letter, declaring she was determined to keep going and had been accepted for trials with a new medication that showed promise.

ALS, or Lou Gehrig's Disease, strikes people right in the prime of life, usually the late thirties or forties. It is an autoimmune condition in which the body attacks its own myelin sheaths around nerves and destroys them so impulses cannot be sent to the voluntary muscles. Slowly she lost the mobility of hands and arms, then feet and legs and could not walk. She started this phase with a motorized scooter, then a motorized chair, and at last with a special version that allowed her to raise the seat to be seen behind the altar.

Finally the muscles that control speaking failed her. It used to be that a person with ALS entered permanent silence at this point, although the mind was fully active and aware. The unmerciful disease traps a person's mind in a helpless body that cannot respond. It is a condition that could justifiably send a person into despair. Now a voice synthesizer is available. It can be controlled by motions of the head and eyes directed at a screen mounted on the chair. And this is what she did, introducing us to her new voice. With it she continued to conduct services, preach sermons, attend to parish duties, and visit the sick.

It became apparent to us that as her physical abilities decreased and she grew weak in body, something else increased. Forgive the Irish in me, but I cannot describe it in any other way but as a glow, an incandescence. It was in her face and eyes, and it was getting stronger. No one dared miss a Sunday or any other event at which she was present. We needed to be near her because she made us near to something indescribable. I remember staring at her, that beautiful woman with a mass of blonde hair and blue eyes so full of light.

During those three years, almost the whole parish made the trip to a nearby city each October to be part of her team in the ALS walk, a fund-raiser for medical research of the disease. We followed her around the track, she in her wheelchair leading the way. We raised great amounts of money and usually had the most team members present. We needed to stay right next to whatever she was.

We will not be going this October. Or, at least if we do, she will not be at the head of the parade. Two weeks before the beginning of Lent, she made the announcement that she was no longer able to serve us officially. Several days earlier she had lost the use of the muscles in her neck. That meant she could not operate the head pads that ran her wheelchair, and she could not direct the silver dot on her forehead at the synthesizer screen to make it speak. She could also not swallow now.

The neutral substitute voice told us this. Her face told us the version with tears. Sobs came from throughout the congregation. We knew it was coming, but we hoped it would not.

In the foyer afterward, we each said good-bye. We are a hugging parish, but this time we hugged carefully. She had become so crushable. And yet her face glowed throughout this, the shining silver dot now useless on her forehead. She did not try to speak with it.

This is my last image of her, a still figure in a white alb and radiant face, despite the tears. We should have been taking care of her, but she took care of us. She brought us to a thinness where something really important kept breaking through, and we could not bear to lose that. The terrible disease brought out what cannot fully be described. It drew us to her.

Two weeks later, on Ash Wednesday, she died peacefully at home. The funeral was huge. Not only our whole parish but also friends and clergy from all over were there. The parking was like for a rock concert. She would have laughed at that. Her family carried in the urn and placed the handkerchief pall over it. Under the stand they set a pair of her red rhinestone slippers, so she could find her way home. We hung onto that thought.

Snow was on the ground. The weather had been miserable all week. That day it cleared and the sun shone. We were not surprised. She was buried in the churchyard near the path to the little chapel which she so often traveled in her motorized chair to conduct early morning services. She had done so that last Sunday, almost unable to make it because of her weakness. But she arrived at the last minute, determined to finish what she set out to do.

Three months have passed. All who knew her grieve. The glow is fading. Please do not misunderstand. Our memory of her does not diminish. She is still overwhelmingly in our thoughts. The effect of her work with us continues to be evident. When we look at the places we grew accustomed to see her and find them empty, we still see her in our minds. But the place is just a place. What I mean is that the physical location is not the thin place here. The thin place was her.

This happened in a church community with a clergy member, and some will say we were biased toward accepting what cannot be verified by the rules of physical science. But many people outside that community experienced the special quality and remarked upon it. There are too many stories to discount. And those who tell them cannot all be Irish.

People new to the parish will find it loving and welcoming. They will be surrounded by what soon feels like family. It is a good place. They may have transfiguring moments, epiphanies, life-changing events in this place. But if they did not have the chance to be there when she was there, they will not experience the particular and unusual luminosity I describe which was associated with her. The location was not the thin place allowing it in. It was her.

She has a name, but I shall name her Iona, after that rugged speck of island where exhilarating things happen. It is also in honor of a legacy that invites me into thin places when I find them and acknowledge they exist, despite the lack of more solid evidence. It is a reminder to let thinness change me. My grandmother smiles at this.

The Rites of Spring

Erin Newton Wells

(First place nonfiction, *Skyline* spring contest, 2015)

May is the month that says all is finally well. Warmth and color return after a winter of snow, a March and April of false starts. It is the friend you can trust. But years ago I learned of a shadowed part that hides toward the end of this favored month behind the blooms and blue sky. It is never welcome, always a surprise. Just when things couldn't be better, it steps out to demand its due and break the hearts of so many people.

I stand before a small group of high school students on the first of May.

"Who knows what day this is?" I ask them, as I have asked their predecessors over the years.

"Monday?" someone finally offers.

"No, I mean what's the significance of the day?"

The less polite visibly roll their eyes. The rest do so inwardly. But no one ever gives the answer I seek. They hunker down, waiting to get back to the lesson.

But, of course, this is the lesson. Officially our time together is listed as Art on their schedules. And yet I forever point out to them that my seemingly random wanderings are going somewhere of importance. When they ask what they should study to prepare for a career in art, I answer, "Everything. Everything." Nothing is too small or unrelated.

"It's May Day," I say, supplying the answer one more time.

More blank looks. So I begin to tell them of its history, far back when people were in touch with the land and were truly exuberant as the season of growing returned. They spent the day outdoors, sang, feasted, danced around a May pole, made garlands of flowers and crowned a Queen of the May. Literature has numerous references to it, and many customs descend from it. It often appears in art. It is part of what makes us a species with a remembered culture.

"Did any of you make May baskets when you were younger?" I ask. But I already know the answer.

They look up, preceded by the snapping of cell phones under the table. Use of the phones is forbidden. It is like asking them not to breathe.

"When I was a little girl, we made baskets of a piece of paper rolled into a cone. A paper strip was attached for a handle."

The heads drop down again. In earlier times this posture would indicate guilt or extreme humility. Now it is the pose of texting. Fleeting smiles pass across faces as they check gnomic postings from virtual friends.

"We gathered flowers from our yards to put in the baskets," I continue, "then hung them on the front door knobs of neighbors. We rang the bell and hid to watch as they found the gift."

At least one girl gazes into space, as if she might be thinking about what I said.

"This simple custom comes from those earlier times," I conclude. "It ties us to those people."

Her head drops. One of them asks permission to go to the bathroom. The others start shuffling materials, setting up their drawing boards. It's the same as having the Vaudeville cane reach out and pull me off the stage. Vaudeville. Another topic they don't know.

I put the example of a standing figure on a display easel. I haven't told them yet about the complete reversal of the old May Day to the May Day parades of the Cold War era. The Soviet Union's marching soldiers and rolling stock of missiles and tanks turned it into a celebration of military might, not the joy of spring.

There's the May festival of my childhood, too. We danced at a May pole in the school yard. I want to tell them this. But as I look at these gifted children sprawled around the table, I see the high school of my senior year, and the shadow hovers at the edges of the room. If only I could push it back until it never came out again.

These days the school year often runs into June. But May was the end in my school days, the month of graduation. We had no air-conditioning in the schools then, and I grew up in the South, in the state as far south as you can go without bumping into Mexico or sliding into the Gulf. School finished by Memorial Day of necessity, before the miasma of real summer set in. Along with graduation came prom night in the latter half of May. We felt relief we would soon be free. It was time to celebrate. But there were always some who let it get out of control.

At least where I lived, we didn't have those contained after-prom parties now offered by many communities. Groups of us hosted our own parties or went somewhere to celebrate together, like the famous pizzeria in town. But there were also carloads that traveled the short distance across the border of our dry state into the neighboring wet one. This meant a lot of teenagers behind the wheel with their minds on anything but safety. Returning late that night or in the dark hours of the next morning, their minds were even less capable of concentrating on the road.

I'll call her Marion, like the Queen of the May in Robin Hood's forest. Every school has a Marion. This group in front of me, for instance, surely can name someone like her. She is pretty, sweet, takes part in everything, makes top grades, a class leader, and the most likely to succeed at being Marion forever.

The Marion of my senior year was in Latin Club with me and in Honor Society, too. But she kept going where I left off. A class officer, a member of the homecoming court, she had it all, including Deke. I'll call him Deke, the basketball star, math whiz. They'd been the perfect couple all through high school. We expected to see them happily married someday and leaders of the community.

At the pizza palace after the prom, some of the others persuaded Marion and Deke to go along with them over the state line. Anyone could see they didn't want to. But, hey, the others said. Once in a lifetime have some fun. They left, and the restaurant emptied out a bit.

I look at my superior students who have made it all this way through school. They are at work drawing figures in motion, and they check proportions with their fingers the way I've taught them. They use the unit of a person's head to plot the body. They learn to ask themselves how many heads it takes to measure someone. When people who don't know me ask what I teach, I tell them Life. It is what makes the figures move as these students sketch. Hang onto Life, I say. It is an important subject. You will need it.

If they would listen, I would like to tell them that the story turned out well. I would like to say that all of us met up again at school on Monday to laugh and wink as we shared tales of the magic May night. But it didn't work that way at all. The shadow hiding among the blooms at the end of spring stepped out and named its price.

The car carrying Marion and Deke swerved on a country road, coming back from across the border. Maybe it turned to avoid a cow that stepped out just then or to miss a slick stretch after a light rain. Or there was fog. Or the driver didn't notice anything at all by that time, and his hands just turned and turned the wheel any which way, once in a lifetime.

It was Marion and Deke in the backseat who were thrown from the car and killed when it swung around and slammed the rear end on a pole. No one had seat belts back then.

There was no joy that Monday, after we heard the news. The May queen was dead, along with her king. Innocence went directly out of my life. Two were missing at the graduation ceremony that year. How many seniors does it take to equal a graduating class? How many Marions and Dekes to make the world go round again?

Almost every year since then, usually in May or close to it, I will hear of another tragedy like this. Sometimes it is in the town where I live now. But it can be found in news notices from all over this country, those brief statements of names we don't know and places we haven't been. Teenagers joyriding after proms or graduation parties meet up with the same shadow we all have learned to know so well and wish we didn't.

I want to pound on the table to get the attention of these bright students in front of me, some of them about to graduate this year and the others not far behind. I want to tell them to put their assignments aside for a moment, to let their thumbs be silent on the messages they think I don't see them

144

making below eye level. Let the brain static not interfere with what I have to say.

Continue through this May, I would tell them if they would listen. Outlast it, and another and another spring, until you are old enough to see a younger generation roll its eyes at the stories you tell of your own youth. Do not be consumed this year by the rites of spring, I would say.

Last Treasures

Gary D. Kessler

(Third place nonfiction, Blue Ridge Writers VWC, 2015)

How do loved ones cut their possessions down to last treasures when being forced into progressively smaller living spaces over the years? What priorities do they set in choosing what to keep and what to part with? What do their choices say about their essential character? And how do those who remain keep these last possessions from becoming a lost treasure?

As I was writing this opening to a short story, I realized that this question had plagued me since the day my mother, aunt, sister, and I descended on my grandmother's room in a Franklin, Indiana, Masonic rest home with a half hour only to retrieve mementos after her death. We had to leave within that time for her funeral in a town several hours' drive to the north, and the rest home was giving us just one "go" at retrieving and dividing personal belongings. What was salvageable from the rest would go to the home's secondhand store that supported its entertainment programs.

I was on edge and barely containing an anger that wasn't reasonable, but nonetheless was real. The room was small and sparsely furnished and decorated. But that's not what had me on edge. Neither was it that much of what my grandmother was leaving behind would wind up in a thrift store. There simply wasn't much left, and I didn't begrudge the home needing to finance programs for its residents.

Although my grandmother had lived in nice homes before I knew her—she had been wealthy with large homes in Indiana both in town and at a lake but lost everything but her four children when the 1918 Spanish flu epidemic took her husband and destroyed their insurance company business—by choice she was continuously downsizing from that point.

The first I knew, she lived in a small apartment above a store and across the unpaved street from the Crazy Horse Saloon in Craig, Colorado, where she kept us away from the front windows on Friday and Saturday nights because those were still shoot-out nights at the saloon. I'll admit I found these to be exciting and romantic at the time. Later she lived in a first-floor shotgun apartment, not much more than train car in width, where one room led to the next from the front to the back—which also had a mystery and charm of its own. During two wars, she lived with my family to provide support while my father, her son, was off fighting. And later in life she lived with us once again, for a period, and then with an aunt in Indiana before moving into the Masonic home. Although conditions were Spartan there, ever independent, she had chosen it and enjoyed living where she was much honored into her late nineties as having been some sort of highest-order Grand Dame of the Eastern Star. I have no idea when she'd had time and opportunity to manage that position. She certainly didn't brag about it.

She never had been much for a lot of furniture and the clutter of bric-a-brac in my experience, either. But even what she had noticeably became depleted with each downsizing of her living arrangements, until, in her Masonic home room, there was only a single bed, a rocking chair, a dresser, a braided rug she'd made herself, and two wall-mounted shadow boxes supporting just a few keepsakes.

Multiple issues had me on edge as we descended on my grandmother's last room to glean what we could in the short time we had. First was the feeling of being one of a swarm of locusts, devouring everything in sight in record time, even though the pickings were slim. Second was the price tagging "one of us" was doing as she moved through the room—coupled with her assertion of dibs on whatever she thought had actual monetary value.

"Look over here. Isn't this the bell tree you gave Etta some years back? Remember what you paid for that? Do you really want it back? You must have gotten one for yourself in Tokyo."

"Look, there are her photo albums. As the oldest surviving child, I should get those."

"Oh, she left her wedding rings on the dresser. Those should go down through my branch, since I was the only girl."

"I wonder what happened to the afghans she kept. They should be worth something. She did fine work. She said I should have those."

The other issue that raised my hackles concerned those wedding rings. When I saw them on the dresser, they made me angry—at my grandmother, as senseless and unjustifiable as that was. I had recently made a stopover in Franklin with my wife and kids en route home to Virginia from a two-year assignment in Japan. It was, by necessity of being on government travel orders, a brief filial stop expressly to see Omar—which is what my family had always called Etta, my originally Pennsylvania Dutch grandmother on my father's side. During that short visit, she'd said she had to go to the hospital for some medical tests in the near future but that, yes, it would be good if I could come back after that because I kept saying I wanted to talk to her more about her earlier life. She had been left a young widow with four children and took them from Indiana to Colorado in two Buicks to homestead in the Rockies. To that point, in her Masonic home room, talking about our next visit, Omar, who had functioned as a regional home remedy nurse on the Colorado frontier, had never seen the inside of a hospital, even though she was ninety-seven.

I had forgotten that I'd heard her say earlier in life that she wouldn't go into a hospital until it was time to check out.

And when she'd subsequently gone into the hospital, that's exactly what she did—permanently checked out. It was a family legend that she'd never taken her wedding rings off—that after she'd moved to Colorado as a young widow, she'd had several proposals of marriage and always had just lifted her hand and said she already was married for life. And yet, when she'd gone to the hospital after our stopover visit, she'd left her wedding rings on the dresser in her Masonic home room. She knew, I now realized when I saw them laying there. She knew she wasn't coming back to the room, and she didn't want to risk having her rings disappear at the hospital. Better that they go down the generations in her family.

I felt robbed. I knew it was irrational to be mad at my grandmother. If anything, I should have been mad at myself for not more diligently quizzing her about her early life before then. She'd been right there whenever I'd come home from college, and I was old enough then to know the value of knowledge and research. But I couldn't help it, I felt robbed.

It was while I was staring at those rings and feeling sorry for myself that I noticed what was behind them on the dresser top. There were two chunks of polished, gnarled wood on the dresser. And now that I thought about it, I remembered seeing them in each of Omar's homes. They were pretty ugly, really—thick, twisted wood, the knots of some hardwood tree, neither more than eight inches long, sitting on edge on the dresser. When I looked at the larger one more closely, I could see that two straight pins with red balls at the visible end were stuck into the wood. The smaller piece had no such pins. But, with the reference point of the pins as representing eyes, I could almost see the figures as crudely rendered dinosaurs.

Why would Omar have kept these through all her downsizing moves, I wondered.

I reached out to my mother as she was passing and turned her attention to the figures. "Mother, what are these?"

"Why those are your grandmother's fancies," she answered.

"Fancies? What do you mean 'fancies'?"

"That card, your grandfather," Mother said, pulling me down beside her to sit on the side of Omar's single bed. "Your father's parents went out West every year for extended vacations before the flu epidemic took him. Your grandmother had asthma so bad she was told to go to a drier climate as much of the year as she was able. They had the means then to do such traveling. Well, when I asked about those figures— strange she's kept them to the last—I was told that they went to California one summer—to the ocean beach. He was always the jokester, your grandfather, I've been told. He pulled those two pieces out of the surf and brought them to Etta while she was pinning up her bathing suit. He took a couple of pins from her and stuck them in one of the pieces of wood—see, these pins here. He meant them to be eyes. He told her the figures were her birthday present, calling them California fancies that were all the rage with the rich people out on the coast. For some reason she kept them ever since, and I'm told that, when people came to visit her, she was quick to show them, with a teasing smile, the dinosaur figures her husband gave her that were so prized in California."

My grandfather—my father's father—was a jokester and he and Omar were playful with each other? That was new information to me. Something I'd never known before about my grandparents. I knew there was humor in my grandmother, but my vision of my grandfather was always hazy—and austere. His photos reflect a serious, dignified young businessman. He wasn't smiling even in their wedding photo. His manner of death at a young age couched him in tragedy. This humor streak was family legend I should have found out myself by talking more with my grandmother when there still was time to have such discussions about what her life was like before I was old enough to know her.

Omar was the last of my grandparents—the only one, in fact, I had known personally. At that point, she'd lived in my house for a third of my life, first during two wars and then during my college years. And I only now, after her death, was beginning to learn about her early life—when she was married; when life was young and gay and promising for her—before leveling tragedy struck and she became a struggling, but self-sufficient and independent, frontier homesteader in the Rockies.

Before the year of the Spanish flu, the family had owned an automobile company and helped pioneer that technology. Her husband had won a county treasurer election, only to be struck down three weeks after winning office. She had socialized with Henry Ford and Thomas Edison. Even after moving to Colorado, she had known J.C. Penny and managed one of his earliest stores. I learned that the reason why we had season passes to the U.S. Senate Chamber gallery was because she had saved the life of a Colorado senator. All of this I learned too late to benefit from plumbing the depths of what she had experienced in a significant period of American history. To me, until, too late, I learned she was a lost treasure, she had just been Omar, quietly moving in the background and helping the family cope with its day-to-day activities.

Our time in her room was getting short. She was being buried later that day in Wabash, a few hour's drive north of Franklin. We had to leave for the funeral.

My mother and aunt pressed me to choose a memento or two before we left, although I had hung back long enough that whatever I picked would have little monetary value. My aunt had mined the room well.

Having monetary value wasn't the point, though—at least not for me. I quickly made my choice and we left—with a couple of women present thinking I'd lost my marbles.

Today, there is an oversized teak coffee table in our den—the oversized nature of it having been a mathematical mistake by me when I ordered it made in Bangkok and gave inch measurements in a country on the metric system— oversized so much that when we went house shopping, a must have was a large den to accommodate the coffee table. Spread on the top of the coffee table is an extensive and eclectic collection of wooden figures and doo-dads collected from travels and vacations worldwide. In the center of that collection sit two ugly, "hey what?" gnarled, twisted, and polished chunks of wood that start looking like attempts to depict dinosaurs only when you notice that there are two red-headed pins sticking in one of them to suggest eyes.

I'm pretty sure that no matter how many downsizes I might have to go through in life those two wooden figures will still be somewhere among the last treasures I've kept—just as they were for Omar.

Murder Exposed

Lauvonda Lynn M. Young
(Second place nonfiction, *Skyline* spring contest, 2015)

I am a murderer. My hands have committed atrocious evil. I've been snuffing a wonderful gastric delight. James Putbrese exposed my criminality in his article, "Proper Care and Storage of Cheese" (*Dine, Wine and Cheese*, spring 2015). My heart is weighted with thoughts of the cheese I've sent to the grave.

Everyone in Virginia who reads Putbrese's article will learn about my crime, but Putbrese should be forgiving because he, too, used to kill cheese (page 1). While Putbrese might excuse my gaffe, my friends who know what I've done already are distancing themselves; they glare at me with pursed lips and disdain in their eyes. The contempt I feel keeps me awake at night, and when I manage to fall asleep I have nightmares about deceased cheese. Although I try to keep my murderous hands concealed at all times by wearing gloves, or by cramming the slayers into my pockets, it's impossible. No one is fooled. I might as well tattoo CHEESE KILLER across my forehead. There is no place for me to hide. There has been so much turmoil, I have not been able to enjoy this spring season, my favorite time of the year. It is unlikely I will experience another pleasurable spring; I'm doomed to misery of great magnitude.

There is nothing to be done. My cheese is dead; it rots at the bottom of my trash bin, emitting a smell worse than excrement. Little milk ghosts seek escape as they trawl amid the trash. This is a sad ending for cheap cheese, but it is unconscionable and extremely wasteful for one to discard any portion of a costly, delectable cheese. What was I thinking? There is no doubt in my mind future cheese I purchase will demand retribution for my previous dastardly deeds.

Just as do zillions of other people, I buy tons of cheese. The cheap ones, such as cream cheese or Velveeta, I use as the basis for such foods as soups and macaroni and cheese. Of course, I add other outstanding, expensive cheeses to improve the overall quality of my dishes. The expensive cheeses I splurge to buy fill many needs. When I wish to nourish family, guests, friends, or some of those rich, snooty people I sometimes want to impress, I spend my whole paycheck buying the best and most expensive cheese available at Whole Foods or at The Market located up on West Main Street in Charlottesville. I serve my cheese with other high-cost delicacies and a posh wine. Some of my favorites to serve are Viognier, Pinot Grigio, Italian Chianti, or Trump's Cru. One of my favorite appetizers is spreading a dollop of fig jam on top of a wonderful cheese (such as French Brie, Boursault, or Fol Epi), The cheese and jam is placed upon a delicious cracker. People rave about my wine and cheese.

No use talking about what I've done well, though, because I am a murderer. I can't reverse what happened in the past. I really am a good person, and murdering isn't my forte. I ask for forgiveness.

Putbrese and I slayed our cheese by "wrapping it in plastic wrap" (page 40). I wonder if Putbrese also encased his cheese in aluminum foil, as I often have, an action that no doubt suffocated my cheese. I sure was disturbed to learn I was a killer. Putbrese made me feel a little better, though, after he helped me to understand what the steps I could undertake to save my cheese from an early death. He said, Mahlon Riehl, owner of Cheese World in Harrisonburg, Virginia, says it is best to wrap it in wax paper. He adds, "cheese will last longer" and "a cheese owner can achieve the full flavor of the cheese" when it is "properly wrapped and stored" (page 41).

Further, Putbrese recommends that "cheese should be removed from its original wrapper and re-wrapped in wax paper, parchment or butcher paper." Putbrese adds that the "cheese should be placed in a plastic bag and refrigerated" (page 41). Oh Heavens, my ghastly tragedy could have been avoided if someone had given me this important information earlier in my life. Mountains of money no doubt would have been saved. Maybe I could have bought a Porsche with my savings. Dismal tomorrows sure must be in store for me.

Putbrese made me feel worse when he added, "When you buy a really nice and generally expensive cheese, you don't want to ruin it with a lack of parenting skills" (page 2). It took me weeks to shake the depression that befell me after reading Putbrese's words about poor parenting. Murdering cheese may be common, but this doesn't help me to forgive myself.

There are other things Putbrese lists that will help cheese to survive. He said, "cheese must be able to breathe," (page 41) and added, "breathing cheese will last longer" (page 4). Later in his article, Putbrese noted cheese "should not be sliced until it is purchased and ready to be used" (page 41). Some other things Putbrese said a cheese lover could do to extend the life of cheese are (1) properly wrapping of the cheese, which "properly prevents mold"; (2) "mold spores spread readily, not only to other cheeses, but also" to anything in the refrigerator that is placed near the cheese; and, lastly, (3) Putbrese notes, "cheese should not be placed close to other strong-smelling foods because breathing cheese will absorb other aromas" (page 4). Who knew?

Why didn't someone enlighten me earlier? If I had been informed previously, my cheese would still be alive. I've really made a mess of things. Actually, it's worse. I am a murderer.

May Catfish and April Dog

Leonard Tuchyner
(Third place nonfiction, *Skyline* spring contest, 2015)

April and I couldn't have chosen a better day to go fishing. It was, in fact, our first fishing spree of the season. That early Virginia spring day we cast our gossamer line into the waters of Lake Saponi. Early morning sunshine drenched my winter-weary back with waves of warm ecstasy, melting off an early morning chill. Dogwood trees, festooned with white blossoms, seemed to pirouette out of the woods. Oaks were just beginning to leaf. That made it official. Jack Frost had gone back home, and we wouldn't have to see him again for at least seven months.

Raucous, honking Canada Geese had already had their start-of-the-day conversations and seemed pretty well settled in and content to ply the lake waters for sustenance. But once in a while something would get them all agitated and up in arms. They made an impressive racket.

Bumble bees, honey bees, sweat bees added their droning, buzzing timbre to insect shenanigans, as they danced around perfumed colors. Jonquils had given way to orange lily spikes, and. short field violets were too pretty to be mowed.

April and I stepped out on the old wooden dock. She knew the routine, having been fishing with me many times before, and was coming with me whether I liked it or not. There were three imperatives in her life. They included swimming, protecting her flock (which was her family of three humans), and love. She was a big shaggy dog, and as far as I could figure, her lineage included Labrador retriever and collie. April had already proven that she would face potentially lethal dangers to be with her family and to protect it. This was one dog who showed an uncanny understanding of how to please and had an insatiable desire to do so. Of course, when she was going through her adolescence, there were times my wife and I could have killed her for the troubles and tribulations she put us through. The same could be said for almost any teenager, two- or four-legged.

There was just enough breath in the air to keep it alive. Surface water barely showed a ripple.

"Look, April. See those little bubbles popping on the water?"

She cocked her shaggy head, and I knew she could hear them.

"Well, you know what that means. That means there are live things down there. They could be just about anything. They could be tadpoles. Or they could be perch, or catfish, or, or . . . let's throw in a line and find out."

She looked at me quizzically. I knew she understood and was as anxious to find out what our lake would bring as I was.

"Now, we're gonna use the smallest hook and bobber I've got. I have a feeling there's just little stuff down there. Besides, it's probably past their breakfast time."

So I skewered a tiny garden worm on my teeny hook and gave it a light, twitching cast off my spinning reel, and waited.

"You don't mind waiting, April. Do you?"

She was lying on her stomach looking down at the bobber. No, she didn't mind waiting.

"You know, girl, there are different kinds of waiting. There's the waiting on line at a grocery store. That's drudgery, because you know exactly what's going to happen. There's no adventure in that. You just can't wait till it's over."

My friend wasn't listening. She was too busy being in the now, staring at that bobber.

"Then there's waiting for a bite. All your attention is focused on a possibility. A slight sign. The ghost of a nibble. The almost imperceptible dip of a bobber. Now that's adventure. Don't you agree?"

But April still wasn't listening. I was preaching to the choir, when I should have been doing what I was preaching about, like my dog was.

For the most part, those ghost nibbles remained ghosts. I began to wonder if the bobbings were just phantoms in my mind, creations of a desperate wishful thinking. Maybe those tiny bubbles in the water were only swamp gas.

But suddenly: "Hey, April! I got one! I got one!"

She didn't look too impressed, especially when a sunfish the size of a silver dollar emerged, gracelessly dangling off the tip of my hook. I apologized to the cute little thing and returned it to the lake as fast as I could. I swear it gave me the finger as it dove away. A neat thing to do if you're a fish. I couldn't blame him or her.

There were a few more of those shameful experiences before April and I had a powwow and decided to move our fishing location. By that time, she was lying on her side, apparently having lost interest in our pitiful fishing expedition.

"I think the water is too shallow here and maybe too warm. Let's try working our way around the lake to deeper areas. There might even be a catfish lurking around down there in the depths. What do you think, girl?"

She just yawned at me. So I took that to mean, "If you say so."

Before we sashayed on our way, I changed my rigging. Off came the bobber, replaced by a lead weight, and a much more substantial hook was deployed. Always the prepared fisherman, I had a small hunk or two of smelly leftover chicken that had turned into carrion. Humans love to eat the meat of scavengers like crabs and catfish.

April was happy to move. She had become bored, though she would have been willing to lie there on the dock until it rotted, if I were willing to do the same.

We worked our way around the bank without anything to show for it except sunburn. Eventually, we came to a rather steep sloping area where sidestepping was the best form of locomotion. It flattened out a little just before the water's edge. The sun was high in the sky, and it was getting on the hot side of fry.

April decided to go for a swim. As I mentioned, she was a serious swimmer. Her idea of a dip was to doggie paddle across the five-acre lake and back again. If I had been sure there was no one watching, I'd have joined her, skinny-dip style. Instead, I just waited for her return and safe berthing. No sense in getting her tangled in the line on her way back. That dog would have floated with her head comfortably at breathing level, even if she stopped paddling and took a snooze. Her thick shaggy hair was a life raft that could have kept her afloat forever.

Our resident geese were not so enamored by the sight of a swimming carnivore loose in their watery habitat. Wing flapping and hysterical honking ensued, as they hastened to increase distance between themselves and April. To tell you the truth, she couldn't have cared less. Hunting wasn't her thing. Mostly, she was a water-crazed shepherd.

After she got back and had soaked me with her water-shedding shaking, I finally got to throw out my line. My dog waited on top of the bank, looking down at me. I was about to call an end to this day of wonderful futility when . . .

"HEY! We got one! We got one! It's a monster!" My rod bent almost to its limit. I immediately loosened the drag on my reel so the light fishing filament wouldn't snap. I had to let this whopper have some play, but not enough to let him wedge himself behind a rock. If that happened, I might as well cut my line and wish the behemoth luck in getting free. I could feel him trying that trick, but I kept changing the angle of my rod and moving along the bank to make things difficult for him. He was getting closer and closer to the shore, and fighting like a tiger . . . or a catfish. Every inch of the way.

"Wow. Would you look at that? It's got to be at least a foot and a half, at least."

I grabbed the line at the end of the rod to slow down its wild bending and springing. This behemoth kept fighting, suspended in midair by its mouth. I began to stumble up the slope, eager to get him on flat ground where he couldn't flop back into the lake.

"Oh darn," but I didn't say "darn." Somehow, halfway up the hill my fish worked his way off the hook. My worst fears were being realized. He was rapidly squirm-flopping his way down the hill.

"Damn, April. I'm gonna lose him."

I wanted to grab him, but that stiletto spine was sticking up and I knew it was needle sharp. It had to be around four inches long. I didn't want to be stabbed, and I knew how slimy catfish were. So I tried to soccer kick him up the hill. But the bank was too long. He sailed about three-quarters of the way up and was on his way down again, flipping, flopping, and sliding. I swear he was also growling. So I kicked him again. This time his spine went all the way through my canvas shoes and I knew I'd be hurting for a long time. Nevertheless, I was ready to give him another whack when he came at me again. It was gonna be him or me. But before we had our third clash, good old April went into action. She walked calmly down the hill, and grabbed the fish gingerly but firmly with her teeth behind his spear, carried it up the hill, and laid it down beyond its flip-flop range. Then she looked at me in a way that clearly said, "That was fun. Now can we go home?"

I couldn't have agreed more. So I gathered up my fishing stuff and limped along as she carried our prize. It was still given to fits of dangerous wiggles.

When it was sincerely dead, I dressed it out, and that evening my family ate a delicious fish dinner. Except for April. She was never partial to fish.

* * * *

It wasn't long afterward that fishing lost its allure for me. That creature wanted to live. It wasn't just a mechanism full of fighting reflexes. I'd dressed down hundreds of fish in my life time, and I was gradually changing my mind about whether they were capable of fear and suffering. My doubts clouded my enthusiasm, even though I tried to talk my way out of that doubt.

I suppose catch and release would be a lot less painful. Maybe someday I'll try it. But not this year.

As for April, she's long gone now. I often think of her. Everything I said about her in this memoir is not exaggerated. I guess I'll always miss her.

A Passing World

Leonard Tuchyner

Little swirling dust devils of crisp, brown, late-autumn leaves played games of frolic in the sharp morning air. I had to figure out what I was going to do with this Sunday morning. Tomorrow I'd be back at Chancellor Avenue School, trying to survive seventh grade.

A cold New Jersey wind cut through my unlined leather jacket, forcing my teeth to clatter like castanets. I raised my coat collar around my neck and hunched my shoulders against the biting breeze. I stood for a few moments on the sidewalk outside my two-story duplex, looking down the street, where a major throughway ran from one end of Irvington to the other. I didn't like that road at all. It was like a dirty river that was inundating all the good things that my hometown used to be and transforming it into parking lots, buildings, and noisy traffic. I remembered when the street I lived on was called Bull Terrace. It was aptly named because, across the intersection where there was now a Grand Union, were fields of grazing cattle, skirted by woodland, alive with the gurgle of a stream. As little kids we would spend clandestine hours there shooting off firecrackers and playing cowboys and Indians. An hour's trek along the stream would lead me to Union, two towns away from Irvington. They'd changed the name of our street to Nesbit Terrace when they decided to build Stuyvesant Village on the grazing lands.

Well, I still had to decide where to go. I walked to the curb, past the old maple tree growing in the narrow grass strip along the sidewalk, and set off across Nesbit Terrace. Inadvertently, my eyes noticed the huge scar left from the tree's severed limb, where a passing truck had ripped the branch off the maple's trunk—another casualty of progress. I crossed to the west side of the street where the morning sun was not blocked by houses and trees. The warmth bathed my face in a radiant pool of pleasure.

I descended a three-block downhill stretch of broken sidewalk that ran along Central Avenue. Halfway to the bottom

160

of the hill loomed a staid old house that stood atop a tall rise. It looked down from its height disapprovingly at the changing neighborhood. A triple flight of iron-railed concrete steps spoke of inapproachability. I remembered climbing those steps two years earlier, selling packets of flower seeds for the school. I plied the knocker of that imposing door with some trepidation, hoping no one would answer. I was surprised by the kindly old woman who bought several seed packets. But now, there was nothing around the house to soften its austerity—no trees, bushes, or open spaces.

Just beyond the old house was an ugly pair of concrete tenement buildings. They shared front and back yards. Cracked and buckled concrete lay uninvitingly where grass should have grown. The gray desolation extended between the companion buildings to the courtyard in back.

It was not that these blemishes had not existed before the neighborhood changes. But now blemish was becoming the norm. Two of my friends, Michael and Evelyn, lived in this complex, but neither of them appealed to my yearning for companionship on this day.

I thought of visiting Evelyn for a moment. I remembered her when we were both smaller and innocent. I remembered how fast she could run and how comfortable it was to spend time with her. Her gold, braided hair and smooth, clear skin were beautiful to me. But I hadn't seen her for a long time. The last time I did, her skin was blemished with red pimples that were accentuated against her light complexion. She refused to look at me, as though she saw the imperfections reflected in my eyes. I was embarrassed and confused by my feelings. The old comfort we used to feel was gone. A light had vanished from her eyes. To make it more befuddling to me, I realized that if she had become beautiful in the way that developing girls often did, I would be even more embarrassed.

It wasn't only the changes that were taking place in my neighborhood that made me feel like I was losing my home. It was also the changes that were happening inside. I wasn't prepared for them. I was no more comfortable in my skin than Evelyn seemed to be in hers. The world had felt softer, more beautiful, and definitely simpler as little as one year ago. So I decided that I did not want to run into Evelyn. I didn't want to have anything to do with her tenement, which I was not even sure she still lived in. For some reason I didn't want to spend my morning with Michael, either. I just wanted to get away from the concrete.

I crossed the highway to a vacant lot nestled between the Grand Union parking lot and Stuyvesant Village, where my friend Irwin lived. In the middle of that piece of ground was a mountain of piled dirt left over from construction. That giant dirt hill was barren, but the surrounding lot was verdant with weeds and grass. The green was soothing. I climbed to the top of the well-packed mountain of dirt and remembered the previous winter when it had been snow-covered. Several boys had ridden their sleds down the short, but precipitous, face of the little mountain, congratulating themselves on their bravery. I did the same, sitting on the sled with feet forward. Michael was the only one who went head first. I envied him his courage. I never thought of him as brave, and I was uneasy thinking of him that way. He should have been more frightened than the rest of us boys. He was only Michael, son of a meat cutter.

Suddenly, I jumped and slid down the steepest side of the little mountain, leaving gouges from the heels of my leather shoes. I had decided to visit Irwin in Stuyvesant Village. I was headed in that direction anyway. I hoped he was at home, because I didn't want to be alone on this morning with my strange discomforting thoughts.

So I continued west until I came to one of the entrances to his courtyard, which was surrounded by four apartment buildings, each one comprised of four apartments. But instead of turning onto the entrance, I felt a compulsion to continue on my walk, which would take me past the village.

Just beyond that housing development there was a patch of land that still remained unspoiled and unchanged. I needed to see this place again. It was a part of the world that fought desperately to remain a piece of reality. It was a realm of autumn grasses and field bushes. Some of the dried grasses were taller than I, yellow and stiffly moving in the swirls of wind. Skeletal bushes with naked branches rose even taller and formed breathtaking sculptures in the cobalt blue sky. A large brown-and-tan bird whizzed briefly over the fields before disappearing into the brush, its chittering, warbling pronouncements following.

Fifty yards away, an old, squat, dilapidated, abandoned shack stood, framed on one side by an ancient, bare, twisted tree. Yellowish-gray siding blended poetically into the straw colors of the fields. A wood-shingled roof held bravely to its task of protection, even if rotted patches exposed its growing failures. This old house stood humble and brave against the merciless world of progress.

Here was the battleground: the dried grasses and shrub brush protecting the venerable house on one side, and the red grouted brick of Stuyvesant Village on the other. The two armies were separated by a narrow no-man's-land of mowed grass.

I looked longingly at the old place. Timid steps took me to the perimeter of that natural world. A chrysalis bound itself defiantly to the underside of a stunted tree branch, suffering the harsh cold wind. I felt satisfaction in the knowledge that the chrysalis would prevail against the cold and that the dormant life inside would break out in spring.

I took three steps into the field, intending to approach this old, mysterious, gentle place, but something stopped me. I felt myself to be but a brush stroke within a painting. I was in a world that had become only a memory—a doomed, lost world that would only hang as a picture, a trophy on the wall in an apartment of Stuyvesant Village. I had no words for my feelings, but I found myself backing out of the field, reverently, tearfully. The chrysalis hung again before my eyes, and I reached out to break it off and bring it back with me. But I couldn't. My hands were trembling. It wouldn't be right. This piece of promised life belonged here, not in the new world I inhabited.

Then I remembered that I was standing on a narrow strip of mowed grass that was the boundary between this brick-and-mortar village and this older, more innocent world. It was a no-man's-land. I gazed longingly at that passing world.

I let its essence burn itself into my eyes and all my senses. I willed it to etch an indelible image within my heart, so that there would be at least one place in the universe where it would not perish.

Then I turned and walked away. I did not call on Irwin or anyone else that day.

The Warm Springs

Martha Jean Lancaster

It was perhaps early in the spring when the young Indian traversed the Allegheny Mountains. He journeyed to represent his peoples at the council gathering on the Great Water. In the dark of night he found himself in what European settlers would later call the Warm Springs Valley. An evening star's reflection in clear water of a spring bubbling up from the ground beckoned him. Too weary to continue, he eased down in the mineral-laden pool to refresh himself. His renewal was so evident at council that "no other warrior was more graceful in address, more commanding in manner, or more sagacious in council."[1]

Whether this legend was truth or fiction, the story has been intriguing visitors to the Warm Springs, Virginia, since the colonization of Bath County in the far western region of the state. Just as the spring season rejuvenated the soul, the Warm Springs refreshed those who took the waters.

The secret could be in the terrain of the valley, where surface waters drain into the ground and reach depths with higher temperatures than the ground level. The warmer water absorbs greater amounts of minerals from the rock strata below the earth's surface. Filled with nitrogen, the water rises bubbling to the surface.

There are other suppositions as to the heat of the water. One visitor noted the theory of a fellow traveler: "Oliver has already discovered, to a positive certainty, that this valley has been neither more nor less than the crater of a volcano; which is doubtless the reason why the waters of it are so warm. He has picked up several substances, that have evidently undergone the action of fire, whether from a volcano, some neighboring forge, or lime-kiln, I leave it to my masters, the philosophers, to discuss."[2]

An octagonal Gentlemen's Pool House was constructed in 1761. In the early 1800s a Scottish visitor described the spring as "a most Copious one indeed. It forces itself up with great Violence by different issues which Cover a

Considerable Span of ground & the run from which when Collected is Sufficient to turn a Grist Mill. . . . The Water is very clear & transparent, but has a bluish Cast & a pretty Strong Sulpherous [sic] Smell. . . . People who bathe in it Say they experience a most agreeable Sensation."[3]

The Warm Springs Hotel was built about 1810. By then, the springs were a renowned source of medicinal healing and were part of the spa circuit for those seeking respite from summer heat. Each spring resort was reputed to cure different illnesses. Physicians touted its mineral components and prescribed drinking the water as a tonic. The liquid acted as an aperient, or laxative, a diuretic, and as a relief from the symptoms of dyspepsia or indigestion.

If hotel guests did not have their own physician's prescription for the curative aspects of taking the waters, Warm Springs Hotel innkeeper Colonel Joshua Fry would provide them with recommendations from several well-known physicians who had assessed the waters.

In that era guests would arrive in a horse-drawn carriage or stagecoach that would barrel down the Mountain-Valley Road. The carriage rounded the last hairpin curve and there ahead the hotel and the domed top of the pool house rose up in view. The horses slowed as they rounded the fountain in the circular drive and stopped abruptly in front of the expansive three-story brick hotel.

Numerous letters with animated descriptions by guests survive today. One famous visitor in 1818 came away, however, with a negative impression. When Thomas Jefferson journeyed to the Warm Springs, he wrote his daughter, Martha, that he "tried once today the delicious bath and shall do it twice a day hereafter." That first week he bathed three times a day for fifteen minutes per session. He did comment on a "table very well kept by Mr. Fry and every thing else well . . . but little gay company here at this time, and I rather expect to pass a dull time."[4]

The second week he felt "the seeds of my rheumatism eradicated, and desirous to prevent the necessity of ever coming here a 2d time, I believe I shall yield to the general advice of a three week course. So dull a place, and so distressing an ennui I never before knew." The third week of his treatment he wrote, "A large swelling on my seat, increasing for several days past in size and hardness disables me from sitting but on the corner of a chair. Another swelling begins to manifest itself today on the other seat." And, finally, "I am lately returned from the warm springs with my health entirely prostrated by the use of the waters."[5]

A granddaughter of Thomas Jefferson, Septimia Randolph Meikleham, received a letter from a close friend who was staying at the Warm Springs in 1833. The "water gives life and animation to a prospect, after your eye has traced the outline of a mountain upon the horizon, you have seen all its beauty, there is no change, but in a river the scene constantly changes, sometimes calm sometimes rough, even its (unclear) ripples seem to dance with life. I wish you had been with me in the bath at the Warm Springs, how we would have enjoyed it together, it is not an artificial bath but a natural spring constantly bubbling up; at first I was quite alarmed there was so strong a smell of Sulphur, the smoke was so great, and there was such a rumbling noise whilst the water was running off, I was in dread of a visit from his Satanic majesty, but very soon I became quite accustomed to it, and enjoyed the bathing excessively."[6]

Two years later, Miss C.M. Sedgwick arrived at the hotel after a sixty-mile carriage ride. In a letter to a friend, she described the scene from her cottage. "Below the main building is a great bath. It is enclosed by a sort of rotunda as much as thirty feet in diameter, and this filled from four to six feet deep with the warm water, at a natural temperature of 96 degrees. No warm bath can be more delicious; the water is bubbling about you, and instead of the beautiful Princess Lorahayda, you may imagine a thousand water spirits dancing and sporting about."[7]

An author using the pseudonym Perigrine Prolix published letters of description that same year. "The place derives its name from an abundant spring of limpid water, containing a small quantity of sulphureted hydrogen, and emitting bubbles of nitrogen, which flows through an octagonal bath, thirty-eight feet in diameter, having the sides of stone masonry, and the bottom of large loose rounded pebbles. It is covered by a wooden building, having a large opening in the middle of the roof to admit air and light."[8]

He advised on the proper bathing attire of "a large cotton morning gown of a cashmere shawl pattern lined with crimson, a fancy Greek cap, Turkish slippers, and a pair of loose pantaloons; a garb that will not consume much time in doffing and donning." Prolix suggested remaining in the pool "fifteen minutes, using very little exercise whilst in the water. As soon as you come out, hurry to your cabin, wrap yourself in a dry night gown, go to bed, cover up warm, go to sleep, get into a fine perspiration, grow cool by degrees, wake up in half an hour, dress and go to dinner with what appetite you have."[9]

The popularity of the springs increased so that a separate Ladies Circular Pool House was built in 1836. Dr. Henry Huntt of Washington, D.C., assessed Warm Springs and called it a "pleasure bath," rather than medicinal, based on its temperature and natural elements. "The water is perfectly transparent, and almost as buoyant as the Dead Sea. Bubbles are constantly rising from the bottom." He stated, ". . . as a bathing establishment, it cannot be surpassed."[10]

Many selected Warm Springs as their summer retreat, including Dr. John Brockenbrough, former president of the Bank of Virginia, who was proprietor of the hotel and pools in the second quarter of the nineteenth century. Author of *The Mineral Springs of Western Virginia* William Burke commented on Brockenbrough. "We hope the nymphs of the fountain will annually seethe him to re-juvenescence, so that for many, many years, he may adorn society as one of the last of the 'gentlemen of the old school'—a generation, now, alas! rapidly passing away."[11]

In the 1850s, travel to Warm Springs must have been similar to anecdotes noted by Mary Jane Boggs, who went by carriage from her home in Spotsylvania County. Her destination was the Alum Baths on the eastern side of Warm Springs Mountain. Mary, her father, and two female cousins transported "two carpet bags, two valises & two band-boxes, besides a trunk behind, which, with the addition of a tin cup for the purposed of drinking on the road formed the whole of our baggage." Their fare consisted of "some cold tongue, biscuits, & sponge cake" prepared by her aunt. They went only as far as Alum Springs, where the party was "drinking as hard as we can & eating right poor victuals too." Apparently they did not take the waters there, as they continued on to Buffalo Gap, Staunton, Weyer's Cave, Charlottesville, and home.[12]

A decade later, the Civil War brought changes to the atmosphere and purpose of the hotel. The medical director of the Army of West Virginia appointed Dr. John Harrison Hunter to "establish a convalescent hospital" at the hall of the warm, hot, and healing springs. It is possible that the Gibson Cottage or others on Cottage Row were used for isolation of patients with communicable illnesses. During that time the Ladies Pool House was adapted, by a request from Mrs. Robert E. Lee, who suffered from arthritis, with a stocky wooden chair that could be lowered into the water for the infirm. The hotel served as hospital and headquarters for both the Southern and Northern troops during the war.

One soldier in the 7th Tennessee Regiment wrote in his diary about their brief stay in the area in 1861. "Warm Springs was a great summer resort, and at the spring they had a large bath house built over the pool, which the warm water ran through. The pool of water must have been about 40 or 50 feet square, and 4 or 5 feet deep. On the side of the pool were little dressing rooms. We all went down there and went in, it felt so good, that some of the fellows stayed so long that when they got out they were so weak they could hardly walk."[13]

After the war, the hotel and pools were on the market in 1871 and advertised as follows: "This ancient and celebrated watering place is noted and esteemed for its medicinal and curative qualities, salubrity [sic] of climate, health-giving and pleasure baths—the baths have no superior in the world. There are now five warm baths of a temperature of 96 to 98 degrees Fahrenheit, and two of them spout baths. . . . The Warm Springs may be safely described as the Paradise of watering places."[14]

In addition, a newspaper notice announced the public auction of the contents of the hotel. The lot of furniture consisted of "135 Mattresses (hair and shuck), 90 Bed steads,

Tables, Chairs, Parlor Furniture, Wash Stands, Blankets, Sheets, Pillows, Bolsters, Carpets, Queensware, Knives and Forks, Spoon, &c. Also, at the same time and place, 10 or 12 head of milch cows, one yoke of large Oxen, about 15 head of 2 year old Cattle, two ox wagons, and a number of other articles not mentioned."[15]

Apparently the hotel was revived by 1873. Owner John Lewis Eubank published a brochure that listed guests from twenty-two states from as far south as Texas, as far north as New York, as far west as Iowa, and from around the Commonwealth of Virginia. He included letters from esteemed physicians who lent their evidence of the healing powers of the waters.[16]

At the end of the nineteenth century the Hot Springs Company purchased the hotel and pools. In competition with the Homestead, Warm Springs Hotel was left to deteriorate and was demolished, being considered a fire hazard, in 1925. The pools are still open today as the Jefferson Pools. The bathhouses along with the one original cottage, the Gibson Cottage, are integral reminders of the refreshing mid-nineteenth-century Virginia spa era. The pools still offer guests a forty-five-minute soak, a spring-like renewal for those want to experience the meditative and restorative aspects of the mineral waters.

Endnotes

1. Oren Frederic Morton, *Annals of Bath County* (The McClure Co., Inc., Staunton, Virginia, 1918), 45–46.

2. James Kirke Paulding, *Letters from the South, Writing During an Excursion in the Summer of 1816. By the Author of John Bull & Brother Jonathan, &c. &c* (James Eastburn & Co., New York, 1817), 135.

3. Sir Alexander Dick, *Journal of Alexander Dick in America 1806–1809*, edited by Helen Beall Lewis (Master's Thesis, University of Virginia, 1984).

4. Thomas Jefferson letter to Martha Jefferson Randolph, August 7, 1818.

5. Thomas Jefferson letters to Martha Jefferson Randolph, August 14, 1818; August 21, 1818; and September 11, 1818.

6. Randolph-Meikleham family papers, 1792–1882, Accession #4726-a, Special Collections, University of Virginia Library.

7. Miss Catharine M. Sedgwick letter published in John Lewis Eubank's *Warm Springs, Bath County, Virginia, In New Hands and Greatly Improved, Open on the First Day of June*, 1873 (Gary's Steam Printing Establishment, Richmond, Virginia, 1873), 21.

8. Peregrine Prolix (pen-name of Philip Houlbrouke Nicklin), *Letters Descriptive of The Virginia Springs; The Roads Leading Thereto, and the Doings Thereat* (H.S. Tanner, Shakespeare Buildings, Philadelphia, 1835), 22.

9. Ibid.

10. Huntt, Henry, M.D., *During the Summer of 1837: With Observations on the Waters* (Duttton and Wentworth, 1839).

11. William Burke, *The Mineral Springs of Western Virginia and Remarks on Their Use, and the Diseases to Which They are Applicable* (Wiley & Putnam, New York, 1842), 64.

12. Andrew Buni, editor, *Rambles Among the Virginia Mountains: The Journal of Mary Jane Boggs, June 1851* (The Virginia Historical Society, Richmond, Virginia, 1969), 82–83, 104.

13. Richard L Armstrong, president of the Bath County Historical Society, "Tennessee Troops March Through Bath," *Bath County Heritage Newsletter*, 2005.

14. *Commissioners' sale of the Warm Springs, a celebrated watering place in Bath County, Virginia* (Virginia Gazette print, Lexington, Virginia, 1871), Special Collections, University of Virginia Library.

15. *Staunton Spectator*, November 7, 1871.

16. John Lewis Eubank, *Warm Springs, Bath County, Virginia, In New Hands and Greatly Improved, Open on the First Day of June* (Gary's Steam Printing Establishment, Richmond, Virginia, 1873), 21.

ON WRITING AND PUBLISHING

Every Story Is a True Story

Jody Hobbs Hesler

"Is this story true? Is it about you?" Almost every time a writer shares her work, someone asks these questions. Leaving aside for the moment the importance of authenticity—a whole different sort of truth—I will answer with a little story about a story, and also about me.

I live in a small neighborhood a couple miles outside the city limits of Charlottesville, Virginia. The stretch of road that separates me from the first stoplight in the city is just long enough to promote a mini-Alpha driving state. Along that road, I pass the Monticello National Guard headquarters, the Charlottesville-Albemarle Regional Jail, a few strips of low-slung brick and cinderblock shops, and some empty lots. The Blue Ridge peeps beyond the edges of everything else, splashing some beauty into all the utility.

On that short drive to town, my mind wanders. I'm a writer; my mind wanders all the time. All my ideas come from the wandering. But one day, my mind wandered the wrong way. I came to that first downtown intersection, my two young daughters in the backseat, and I didn't notice the light had just turned red.

I swerved. Another driver slammed on his brakes. There was no crash, just my quick draw of breath and my heart banging, then a return to our commute, as if nothing had happened.

But what almost happened stayed with me. We could have been hurt or killed. We could have hurt or killed someone else. Whatever would have happened would have been my fault. For months, I couldn't drive through that intersection without shuddering. If the worst had happened, how would I have lived past it?

That question percolated in my unconscious, and scenarios started to bubble up. Different people with different circumstances marched across my imagination, facing similar crises and failing to swerve. A woman about my age, frazzled to distraction by her child's speech impediment and emotional difficulties runs that red light and causes an accident, not with another car but with a pedestrian. How does the mother feel after she injures someone? Maybe she goes to the victim later and tries to make amends. Maybe the victim is an African-American woman, seeing the car driver's attentions as some sort of pathetic race apology. Maybe she develops a kind of affectionate pity for her anyway.

Another story was mucking around in my brain at the same time. I had attended a Thanksgiving family reunion where a misunderstanding had bred ill will, and I wanted to figure out how to write about the strange kinds of allegiances and resentments that grow up in families. From that generic root grew an alcoholic young man, about to join his family's annual Thanksgiving gathering for the first time in many years so he can show off his girlfriend. She embodies everything he thinks is worthwhile about himself. But the morning of the trip, she breaks up with him. By the time he gets in his car, he's cross-eyed drunk. He runs into a woman crossing the street and flees the scene. When he arrives at the family gathering, no one knows what's happened. Much to his surprise, they seem genuinely delighted to see him, even without his trophy of a girlfriend. Then the police come for him in the middle of the night, waking everyone up and arresting him.

Slowly, these two stories morphed into one. I phased out the my-aged woman from the one story, got rid of the family gathering in the other. Lanky, hapless Buckley Sanford took shape. The merged story begins with him fresh out of jail for a drunken hit-and-run accident, hoping to make anonymous amends to the woman he injured. In my mind, the jail he was fresh out of is the very one I pass on my way in and out of town. (The resulting story, "Sorry Enough," will appear in *Gargoyle #65*, Fall 2016.)

Is this story true? Is it about me? Well, I wouldn't have thought of it if I hadn't run that red light. The specters of guilt and remorse I glimpsed in my not-quite-tragedy I gave in full force to Buckley instead. The setting I pulled from my daily life, too, choosing specific, familiar parts of town to locate the accident and the places where my characters live and work.

The intersection that used to make me shudder transformed into the place where my real life and my characters' imagined ones intersected. My feelings about those characters deepened with every pass I made over those roads. It was a sad place because the hit-and-run victim, Ida gets hurt pretty badly, and Buckley is never the same.

"Is this story true?" It seems like such a simple question, and the simple answer is, "Yes." Every good story is true, just not always in the way the asker imagines.

Less Is More

Sarah Collins Honenberger

Blogs, texts, e-books—in today's digital world we're inundated with words. In any given minute more people are sharing thoughts on Facebook than were alive in 1900. In this flood of verbal communication, selecting what we say and how we say it matters. Discussion becomes dribble, debate deteriorates into dogma, and the power of words to illuminate or persuade drowns in the never-ending torrent.

I believe in the power of editing. My nickname in writing circles is Fierce Red Pen. When "walking quickly" becomes "sprinting," you feel the urgency. "Worn" becomes "threadbare" and you're chilled. Through deliberate word choice and arrangement writers strive to create lasting images and examine ideas that add to our understanding of what it means to be human. By honing stories so every word counts, so every scene adds to the whole, so every character is three-dimensional and as real as a best friend, I search for the leanest, freshest way to express the actions and emotions of my characters.

I believe in thinking before speaking. To break down ideas into manageable thoughts allows one to fine-tune details that will convince the reader of an underlying truth. Credibility springs from those details. When a reader believes, a reader is listening. Listening yields understanding in a way that the blare and blast of arguments can never achieve. With the wrong words a mother's despair when her son joins a gang or a father's rage at his daughter's rape are trivialized or enflamed. With the right words, that portrayal of fear and rage can mobilize or heal or inspire.

Imagination is a powerful tool. The exercise of imagination during the writing or reading of another person's experiences helps us see the world through someone else's eyes. Empathy is bound to follow. Concern over another's pain, celebration over her joy, discretion, patience break down barriers, whether she hides in a hovel in Afghanistan or lives in a palace in Bangladesh.

As an editor I believe that less is more. Like the North Star, the strongest light guides while the galaxy of stars blur together in the night sky, wondrous, but not helpful. Spewing opinion, without consideration for the language chosen, without deliberation as to how the reader may react, only polarizes. Even a barrage of facts cannot prevail if the words are too many and too fast for assimilation. With modern technology people's opinions are broadcast simultaneously and at earsplitting decibels. In the cacophony events and emotions are reduced to sound bytes, hollow clichés that drone as background to the failure of mankind to make peace or achieve justice. And even more simply to our failure to hear what the other fellow is trying to say.

Communication at the human level is unique to our species. Only humans leave written records of their history, culture, and ideas. And build libraries to preserve those records. That ability needs to be taken seriously. Each word, each story, each book has the power to change the world. I believe in the power of words.

Poetry and Publishing

What Is Poetry?

Poetry is born in fire.

Poetry is born in the image behind your eyes, the one you can't forget but don't know quite what to do with. It comes in the phrase that rings on your ear like crystal, the line that, sounding in your head, is perfect. Working out that image, that phrase, that line—that particular combination of sound and rhythm and meaning—that's where the poem comes into being.

Poetry is born in inspiration. It comes unbidden, in odd moments. It comes in the middle of the night when you wake from a dream that dissolves in mist but leaves you with one firm fragment, like a shard of glass, glittering and dangerous. In the grocery store when you notice a weathered hand closing around a fat apple, and your eye traces a line from apple to hand to face, where the history of one life is written for anyone to read, if only they know to look. In the passing lane on the highway when a hawk on a power line strikes you in silhouette and your heart breaks from the spare beauty.

Poetry is born in fire, but it takes shape in labor. Developing the image, finding the rhythm, tracing the arc and the form, and all of it hard words, hard work in the forge of the mind. Too often the poem sprouts and flourishes but then withers and grows brittle. Too often it limps along line by line, running lower and lower, its tempering weakening, until it rambles off to a conclusion of sorts or it just shatters and falls dead.

Endings are harder than beginnings. In the beginning, the thing is unfinished, unformed. All potential. Putting hand to pen and pen to paper, chasing that potential thing in your head, is work, and easily interrupted by any passerby inquiring the way to Porlock, or the kid wondering where the milk is when it's in the fridge where it's always been, or an associate who thinks you need cheering up with a story about the weekend's softball game and the foul ball that was almost, but not quite, caught. It's work even when you're not interrupted, but picking up that frail thread of concentration and reconnecting to that part of your brain where knowledge runs too deep for words, that place where words are pale echoes of the vivid truth in your head, that's really hard work.

It's also really important work. Not only finishing the vision, but finishing it well, finding the echo of that bell-like beginning. If you talk to poetry editors, one of the complaints you'll most commonly hear is that too often a promising poem starts strong but fades coming into the stretch and limps across the finish line. Weak endings—the bane of poets and editors alike.

Finishing a poem is an art to itself. It requires a deft touch, not a sledgehammer. Punching home a tagline at the end of a poem is a cheap way to finish—it's a shortcut through nettles instead of following the path; it's ungainly and ungraceful, and brings your poem to a bedraggled conclusion. A poem that wanders off or withers on the page marks a poet who has either lost interest or just doesn't know how to do it. Poetry starts in fire, but it ends in steel, and the alchemy is everything between.

Poetry is one of the world's very few vocations that exists truly as art. And it's one of the very few arts where excellence triumphs eventually. Always. The world is full of bad novelists, musicians, filmmakers, and the like. Many are quite popular; some sell very well. But their work won't last, and what they're doing isn't art.

If writing exists on a spectrum (and it does), it's a spectrum that accommodates novels and short stories, essays, sermons, etc. etc. And on the far end—poetry. Poetry is language and meaning distilled to their essence. Poetry is to writing as ballet is to dance. It is by definition art. The oldest and greatest of the arts.

As a poet, you inherit an august tradition, one that stretches back to the beginning of language itself; before writing developed, people cast their history, their law, their culture, and all the work of their minds and hearts into verse so they could remember it. Mnemosyne, mother of the Muses, wept when writing appeared, because memory would no longer be paramount. The Celts kept an oral tradition that revered poets above all others, even priests. Kings brought their poets to battle and, if the army was defeated, only the poet was spared; Aneurin composed *The Gododdin* after such a battle. The oral tradition, rooted in paganism, evaded all efforts to tame it and existed until the eighteenth century in Ireland, when the last of the hedge poets were hunted down, inheritors of a tradition that required, before one could claim the honor of composing his own work, he had to learn everything that came before.

Fortunately, our training isn't quite so rigorous. But the same principles apply. Great poets start out by being good poets and work from there.

If you want to publish, be a good poet.

What does that mean? Well, it means you need to read. A lot. Read out loud. Don't be embarrassed. You already love words, so enjoy them. If you're a poet, you'll be staging readings of your own works, anyway, so you might as well practice. Use a mirror. Tape yourself, watch and listen to the playback. Hear the words and the rhythms—what sounds in your head and what comes from your throat are not the same, and you need both. Your words need to work on both the visual and aural planes. Read poets you like and poets you don't like, and figure out what each group does that works.

Learn your craft. Yes, poetry is art, like painting is art and composing is art. Like the other arts, it has a journeyman phase, an apprenticeship. The Gaelic poets had one and so did the Griots. In every culture, poets-in-training study the form and history of the art. You should, too. Most poets never stop studying it, which is one reason why poets don't retire—it's a lifelong passion, and you only get better with time.

How do you learn your craft? Study prosody and try out what you learn. *A Manual of English Meters* by Joseph Malof is classic and comprehensive. Mary Oliver's *Rules for the Dance* is friendlier and easier to use. I recommend mixing it up. Study meter, rhyme, rhythm. Make a habit of counting syllables and counting stresses, identifying matrix lines—these are the keys that unlock other poets' secrets.

You'll learn that Coleridge was a premier stylist of the line and not a syllable in his poetry is misplaced. You'll find that Keats' mastery of language was surpassed only by Shakespeare, and when you realize that Milton composed *Paradise Lost* in his head before he dictated it, line by line, you'll want to figure out how he did it. You should know that alliterative verse is native to English, and the complex variations of stressed/unstressed beats of *Beowulf* survived in *Sir Gawain and the Green Knight* and Langland's *Piers Plowman*, and on through to T.S. Eliot and into the present day. When you use alliteration properly, you're part of that long tradition. You should know that iambic pentameter is the poetic line closest to normal speech, that there are not enough rhyme words in English to make rhyming easy or natural but Browning will show you how it can be both, that the sonnet is always a love poem, and that the villanelle is one of the hardest poetic forms you can attempt. When you scan poetry (the formal process of breaking a poem into poetic feet or syllable count, identifying the rhyme scheme and stanzaic form, finding the caesuras, the consonance and assonance and all other oddities that make a poem unique—in short, finding the craft behind the art), you'll find that everything has a form—yes, even so-called free verse has form and structure. Learn the secrets of the Beats, the Language Poets, the Metaphysicals, the Romantics and all the rest. Everything you learn becomes part of your tool kit. As you master the craft, you grow the art. You grow as an artist.

Knowing the traditions and the technical aspects of composition isn't just an exercise in pedantry. When you know the tradition you can use it, bend it to your own artistic purposes. You wouldn't build furniture without knowing how to use the tools; building a poetic structure that you hope will outlive you requires no less preparation. When you know, for instance, that the colors of flowers convey meaning and the flowers themselves also hold symbolic resonance, you can use that knowledge to shade your verse, to add nuance, and do so intentionally. Even though much of the magic in poetry operates on the subconscious level, what you do on the conscious level leverages immense power.

You also don't make mistakes, mistakes that reveal your ignorance. You should know that you can't write a waka without referencing its use in traditional courtship. If you use a Madonna symbol, you need to know how to manage the attendant religious overtones. You want to make sure that the sexual subtext you've embedded in the imagery carries a deeper significance, your grace notes of mortality are consciously placed, and that you recognize, unless you're Andrew Marvell, resorting to death threats isn't a great route for seduction.

To this point I haven't written much about publishing. The reason is because publishing has little to do with writing, and writing is more important.

Be a good poet, and you'll publish.

What Is Publishing?

Publishing is your public face. Publishing is not writing. Writing is writing. Writing is where you live. Publishing is something else; it's a shop window, a binocular glimpse at a distant reality. It is not part of you. If you want to publish, I have good news. Do the writing part right, and the publishing part will come.

It may be obvious, but we tend to forget that writing and publishing are different things. If I had a Venn Diagram with two circles, one representing Poetry and the other representing Publishing, the intersection would be a thin slice, indeed. It behooves us to remember that. Not all poets publish. Not all poets want to.

First ask yourself: Why do you want to publish? You need to answer this before you go on. Do you want it for recognition? Fame? Money? (If that's the answer, we need to talk.) Do you write to express yourself? Do you write to communicate? They're not the same thing. Do you want to touch other peoples' hearts, their heads? Do you want to be the next Sharon Olds or Seamus Heaney? If so, then work on your art, work on your craft.

That's the secret. Really. Get good, and the rest will come if you want it.

Despite the unsettled nature of publishing today, despite the pervasiveness of Internet culture and its promotion of skimming instead of reading, despite the chronic underfunding of poetry journals and chapbooks and other venues, poetry is being read and published, enjoyed, loved by readers, and in huge quantities.

As a poet, you read other poets. You attend readings and you talk. You go to poetry conferences. (Yes, such things exist.) You'll be asked to give readings of your own. As your circle of poets widens, you learn about which publications you prefer, which editors you like. You'll meet editors who come to your readings, and they'll solicit your contributions, or you'll submit to them. In other words, it all flows naturally—all you need to do is start, but you start with the craft.

Be a good citizen. We all know poets who exist to express themselves and only themselves. They want to be read but don't want to read. Don't be like them. They're usually unpleasant, and always insecure.

There are basically two ways to see the world of the arts. On one side: The audience is limited. Their attention spans are limited. I need to scrap and fight for my part of that audience. The pie is small and I can't afford to share.

On the other side: Make the pie bigger.

Seriously. If people like what you do, they'll want more of it. They'll bring friends. They'll buy your books. They'll want to read and share your work.

So be a part of your artists' community, but above all: be kind. You'll be happier for it, you'll be more open to the beauties of life, you'll be a better poet, and you'll sleep better.

Submit. Submit. Submit. And then submit some more. Do readings. Attend readings. Volunteer at conferences. Help out. Be part of the community. Let people get to know you. You'll make friends and you'll learn from them. Submit to journals you like. If it doesn't work out, shake it off and submit again. Every time you do, you get better; your art grows and so does your name recognition.

Rejection is not personal, even though it stings. Sometimes it really hurts. We have all felt it. Everyone gets rejected—it's a badge of honor, a battle scar. A printed rejection is better than a nonresponse. A personal rejection is better than a printed one. It means you're making progress.

A rejection is not a dismissal of your work, and certainly not a rejection of you as a person. All it means is that this particular piece isn't right for that particular venue. If your heart is set on being published under a certain masthead, read the publication more and figure out what the editor is looking for. Or find another publication more congenial to your style.

The Internet is your friend. Read your target journal's Web site and follow their submission policies exactly. They're in place for a reason. Check out the editor's Twitter feed. Really. Editors have them. So do publishers and agents, and often they all tweet about what they're looking for.

Finally, if you get a rejection from a publication, but the editor has written something like, "I'd like to see more of your work," she means *Send It Now*. Not in three weeks or two months. It's not obnoxious to follow up immediately. If you wait, your name will have been forgotten. They want to see your stuff now.

Remember to say thank you. To your editors, your publishers, your readers, your mentors, your friends. Remember the people who helped you along the way. Promote them the way they promoted you. Teach others what you know. Share your tools.

There's no denying it, publication is great. It lifts your ego. It's a validation that what meant so much to you means much to someone else as well. But don't get confused—once a poem leaves your hands it becomes a thing in its own right. It will not change your life. Your eyes will get used to seeing the words bound on a page, and then the volume will go on your shelf, and you will move on. Because the poem is not you. You make it, but then you release it to the world, and it becomes something else.

As your reputation builds, you will become aware of a disconnect between your poetry—that is, your persona, and yourself. People will assume they know you from reading your work. You can let them keep thinking that, or not—that's your choice. As long as you remember that you're not your work.

You're the poet, the artist, the wordsmith; the poem is the product.

A poem is beautiful in the way that a flower is beautiful, but the rain that fed it and the soil that nourished it remain, self-renewing and capable of producing new flowers in new seasons. They do what poets do.

Whether you publish it or not; whether you seek, or ever find, acclaim, or not, it's what you do. At the end the poem remains, a monument greater than Ozymandias ever dreamed, ephemeral as mist in the forests of Arcadia, born in fire, finished in steel, a harsh and exacting labor that looks entirely effortless, word and meaning forged into one. Poetry is the writer's highest calling.

Go forth and write.

An Overview of Self-Review

Gary D. Kessler

You've finished writing and getting the words just right in your work. Now what do you need to do with it before you send it anywhere? You should put it through one or more reviews specifically for the presentation issues—format, grammar, punctuation, and spelling—before you either start submitting it to agents or publishers, publish it yourself, or send it to an editor. This process is called self-review.

What Is Self-Review?

First, what self-review isn't. It isn't self-editing (despite the title of one of the resource books listed below). It's impossible for a writer to "edit" him/herself. Only someone else looking afresh at what was written without the preconceived notions of what the writer thought had been written can see some of the grammar, punctuation, and spelling mistakes; inconsistencies; and incomplete connections in a work. The writer will read right through a lot of these because her/his mind is absorbed by what she/he thought was written rather than what actually was spun out on the page. And beyond this, all writers have habitual mistakes they make, and if they made them in the first place, chances are very good they will make them again and never see them on a reread.

What the writer is actually doing when going back through a manuscript to polish it up and correct mistakes is review—"self-review."

And this is something every writer should do even if the work is going to be edited by someone else. The better shape the writer can get the story into him/herself, the fewer mistakes there will be to bog an editor or backup reader down and distract them from seeing other, often more deeply rooted problems in the manuscript.

You can catch many of your own mistakes and polish up your work yourself simply by reading it over again a few times, each time looking at it from a different aspect or for a different issue, before dumping it into the submissions queue, self-publishing it, or sending it to an editor. It may not be a good idea to go over it endlessly, however, because what you may be beating out of it is its freshness and unique and compelling voice.

But you can improve your story a lot by submitting it to three basic read-throughs. Read through it again right after you've written it. You can catch a lot of the surface, glaring structural and presentation mistakes right off the bat. Then, after letting it sit for a while, read it through out loud; you'd be amazed at how many mistakes pop out when you vocalize them that where hidden when everything was still internalized in your brain, where often you just haven't tapped into the file what your brain was thinking. Now, resist the urge to rush your masterpiece to the readers. Put the work aside for a few days and then come back and read it again, this time as much for context as for structure and presentation. As an example, I went over this essay quite thoroughly when I wrote it for a symposium several years ago. But when I reviewed it for this outing, I found three mistakes—and there probably are still even more. There's no such thing as perfect copy.

You've now knocked out of the brain what it chose initially to see that may not really be there—or may not be there correctly. If there are significant contextual, structural, and/or presentation problems, chances are good you will catch the worst of them at this point.

And, by all means, consult resources when you are doing these reads. Yes, put the work through the computer program spell check; just don't expect the spell check's idea of what is wrong or right to be correct. It will, however, pick up a lot of errors that both you and the spell check can agree were typos or errors you just didn't see until you were focused directly on them.

More important, at least have a dictionary at your side (or on your computer desktop) while you read and recheck not just the words that look funny to you but also words you don't use all that often. Recheck to at least one level deeper than you think is really necessary. U.S. publishing mostly uses *Webster's Collegiate Dictionary* for spelling and hyphenation. And it uses the *Chicago Manual of Style* for published fiction and nonfiction in the humanities. But any basic grammar and punctuation book would also be useful to use during your self-review. The *American Heritage Book of English Usage* and Theodore M. Bernstein's *The Careful Writer* are both excellent, easy-to-understand, and useful writer's aids for writing short stories.

Other suggestions are frequently offered on review techniques, like reading the whole story backwards by phrase or word to help you catch spelling mistakes (inadvertent changes in character names can often be caught this way) or scanning through the work looking for certain classifications of habitual problems only (e.g., you/you're and its/it's renderings or overuse of certain words or types of words, like adverbs). On this, though, I counsel the "don't beat all of the life out of it" advice given above.

What Do You Look For?

When you review your story, start with the simple and the obvious, the structural and presentation issues, and work toward the complex, the context. Typically, you won't be able to see contextual problems as long as you are distracted by the more obvious, simpler problems.

Structurally, first look to your paragraphing. Keep your paragraphs for print publishing to not much more than twenty lines of text. For online works, keep paragraphs to about ten lines and put an extra line return between them. Simply scanning through what you've written will show whether you've done this. The dialogue paragraphs should be set apart, with dialogue passages by different characters in separate paragraphs. In American publishing style use double quotes at the first level always and see that those periods and commas and most of the question marks are tucked inside the quote marks. Do all of your paragraphs end with some type of end punctuation? If you use italics, have you done so sparingly?

In a closer look at the story, try to make sure that the **presentation** issues—the grammar, punctuation, capitalization, and spelling—aren't going to distract the reader's attention. Grammar is rough to clean up through self-review, because if you made the mistake to begin with, it's likely a mistake you habitually make and won't see in review. But you can look for subject/verb agreement (singular/plural) and you can try to make sure that sentences have a subject and verb (unless you don't intend them to; in fiction, it's quite all right to have incomplete sentences, as long as you know how to do this to good effect—and not do it all that often). You can also try to make sure that a clause modifying a noun is hung on the noun it actually modifies. (e.g., "I gave my hat, which was red, to you" rather than "I gave my hat to you, which was red").

Try to be consistent in capitalization—and don't try to capitalize every noun in sight; this is a Germanic influence that current English abhors and that can be very distracting to the reader.

And, speaking of "sight," look for those misused homonyms: sight/site/cite, for instance. Mistakes in this category most often not caught in review include you're/your, its/it's, here/hear, their/there/they're, and then/than.

Spelling isn't as much a mystery as most writers think it is—or wouldn't be if they used a dictionary and knew how to use it. The first-listed spelling in a dictionary is the one that's preferred in publishing. And, if the spelling you've found refers you to a different spelling in the dictionary, that different spelling is preferred. Don't rely on Microsoft spell check's idea of how a word is spelled. If it doesn't like your spelling, look it up in the dictionary. Often you were right to begin with. (But also take a look at the meaning; sometimes you will have used a word that doesn't mean what you think it does.)

Look for inadvertently repeated words or prepositional phrases or words dropped. (Unintentionally dropping a "not" can be particularly disconcerting for a reader.)

Simpler words and language and shorter sentences are better than otherwise, unless you are really, really (really!) good at writing.

Microsoft spell check is hopeless at word hyphenation—and so are most writers. Question everything you have decided to hyphenate. The dictionary is quite helpful in this realm. If you don't find the word as a run-on compound word or hyphenated in the dictionary, then it isn't hyphenated. The kicker, though, is that hyphenation of compound modifiers depends on where it is in the sentence—whether it is in an adjective position (ruby-red lips) or behind the verb (Her lips were ruby red). When in doubt, don't (except directly in front of the noun being modified). Elements of compound adjectives that end in "ly" (e.g., "heavily applied makeup") never take a hyphen. (No logic; that's just the way it is in English.)

Publishing uses more commas than is currently being taught in school English courses. When you have a sentence of two independent clauses, they are set off with a comma; but if one of the clauses in dependent, they aren't. Introductory clauses that go more than three words are set off with a comma. Publishing uses the serial comma (e.g., red, white, and beige). All "which" clauses are independent and are set off by a comma; all "that" clauses are dependent and are not set off by a comma.

When your self-review has honed down structural and presentation issues to a level that they won't distract the reader—or you in your self-review process—it would be good to read through your work **contextually**. Are your character names spelled the same throughout? Does the chronology flow properly? Do the causes logically lead to the effects? Are there questions unanswered or story threads left dangling? In a well-constructed story, everything will serve the storyline, the story won't run off on unrelated tangents or dwell on images that don't directly serve the plot. Is what you are trying to say buried in too many words or words that are either imprecise or pretentious? Is this a complete story (beginning/dilemma, middle/action, ending/resolution) if you meant for it to be a story? What's the hook and is it played as well as you think it could be?

Most important, does it flow smoothly to you when you read it aloud? If you get hooked up on an expected or "doesn't quite fit" word, you readers are likely to get sidetracked by it too. If it doesn't go with the flow, change it so that it does.

Resources

Webster's Collegiate Dictionary, 11th edition, for spelling and hyphenation.

Chicago Manual of Style (University of Chicago Press, 2010), 16th edition, for U.S. publishing fiction and nonfiction style.

The Oxford Guide to Style (Oxford University Press, 2002), for UK publishing fiction and nonfiction style.

The *American Heritage Book of English Usage* (Houghton Mifflin, 1996), for grammar/punctuation/word usage.

Theodore M. Bernstein, *The Careful Writer* (Antheneum, 1965), for grammar/punctuation/word usage.

Renni Browne and Dave King, *Self-Editing for Fiction Writers* (HarperCollins, 1994), for self-review techniques.

Leslie Sharpe and Irene Gunther, *Editing Fact and Fiction* (Cambridge University Press, 1995), for editing principles.

Theodore A. Rees Cheney, *Getting the Words Right—How to Revise, Edit, and Rewrite* (Writer's Digest Books, 1990), for self-review techniques.

ABOUT THE AUTHORS

David Black ("Spring Plowing" and "For Plato and My Mother," poetry), a retired English teacher and minister, is a former poetry editor of the *English Journal* and a frequent contributor of poems, essays, articles, and reviews to small magazines and academic journals, especially in the Appalachian region. He is the author of two books, *Some Task, Long Forgotten and Other Poems* and *The Clown in the Tent*.

Leone Ciporin ("Invisible Women," fiction) has published several stories, including four mini-mysteries in *Woman's World* magazine and two stories in the *Chesapeake Crimes* anthology series from Wildside Press. "Invisible Women" was first published in 2012 in *The Hook*, a Charlottesville weekly (now merged into *C-ville*), after placing third in a 2012 contest judged by John Grisham. Leone is a member of Mystery Writers of America and Sisters in Crime. When not writing mysteries, she's a manager at State Farm Insurance in Charlottesville.

Lori Dixon (*Skyline* spring contest poetry judge; "Poetry and Publishing," writing/publishing) wears numerous hats: medievalist, teacher, house restorer, novelist, poet, farmer, long-term cancer patient, decipherer of obscure handwritings, spouse, parent, friend. She gets bored easily and tends to juggle too many projects at once. She lives in a great old house, talks to herself a lot, and practices hack and slash gardening. As the sun goes down, she can most often be found by a fire, next to the river, in good company and with a couple of dogs. She has been honored to judge contests for the Virginia Writer's Club and the Poetry Society of Virginia.

Phyllis Anne Duncan ("Dreamtime" and "Blood and Guts," fiction) is a commercial pilot and former FAA safety official who lives and writes in the Shenandoah Valley of Virginia. Her short stories have been published in the collections *Blood Vengeance, Fences, Spy Flash*, and *The Better Spy*. A novella, *My Noble Enemy*, was published in 2015. Her work has appeared in *eFiction Magazine, Prime Number Magazine, The Blue Ridge Anthology 2013, Skyline 2014*, and in *1 Photo 50 Authors 100 Words*. Her story, "Reset" will appear in the inaugural edition of

The Ink Ribbon Review. She has studied writing at Gotham Writers Workshop, Writers.com, and Tinker Mountain Writers Workshop. She is a member of WriterHouse, James River Writers, Virginia Writers Club, Blue Ridge Writers, Shenandoah Valley Writers, SWAG Writers, and the Association of Writers and Writing Programs.

Stan Galloway ("Sea Door," "Ringtone," and "My Lass in County Kerry," poetry) teaches English at Bridgewater College. He was nominated Best of the Net in 2011, 2012, and 2014, and for the Pushcart Prize 2013. His full collection, *Just Married*, was published in 2013 (unbound CONTENT). He has written two chapbooks: *Abraham* and *A Bird's Life*. He has had more than 100 poems published singly and has also written a book of literary criticism, *The Teenage Tarzan*.

Jody Hobbs Hesler ("Next to the Fortune-Teller's House," fiction; "Every Story Is a True Story," writing/publishing) lives and writes in the foothills of the Blue Ridge Mountains. Her fiction, feature articles, essays, and book reviews appear or are forthcoming in *Gargoyle*, *The Georgia Review*, *Streetlight Magazine*, *Sequestrum*, *South85*, *[PANK]*, *Steel Toe Review*, *Valparaiso Fiction Review*, *Prime Number*, *Pearl*, *Potato Eyes Journal*, *A Short Ride: Remembering Barry Hannah*, *Charlottesville Family Magazine*, and other places. One of her stories was a Pushcart Prize nominee and several have won regional contests, including the Virginia Writers Club Golden Nib and UVa's Writer's Eye, and appear in prize anthologies. Currently earning her MFA in Fiction from Lesley University, she has also enjoyed fellowships at the Virginia Center for the Creative Arts and has conducted writing workshops in area schools for students from third through twelfth grade.

Lois M. Holden ("An Ordinary Day," fiction) lives on the sunrise side of the Blue Ridge Mountains in Nelson County, Virginia. She started writing poems as a child and has continued to write poetry and short stories since those early efforts. She has worked as a publisher, technical writer, book editor, and newsletter editor. Her entry, "Old Sukie and Me," won first prize in the 2013 Fralin Museum of Art (University of Virginia) Writer's Eye competition in the university/adult prose category, and her short story, "An Ordinary Day," received an honorable mention in the 2014 Writers' Eye competition. The short story "The Hearing Aide" won honorable mention in the Blue Ridge Writers Chapter 2014 writing contest. In 2015 her short story, "Target Practice," won third place in the Blue Ridge Writers contest. She is a member of the Lonesome Mountain Pros(e) Writers Workshop, the Blue Ridge Writers Chapter of the Virginia Writers Club, and the Virginia Writers Club.

Sarah Collins Honenberger's (*Skyline* spring contest fiction judge; "Rituals," fiction; "Less Is More," writing/publishing) novel, *Catcher, Caught,* is a Pen/Faulkner Foundation selection in its Writers in Schools program. Audio, German, and Korean editions have been released. With numerous short fiction awards and a fellowship from the Virginia Creative Arts Center, she appears regularly on literary panels and at book festivals. Her other novels include *Minding Henry Lewis* (2014), *Waltzing Cowboys* (2009), and *White Lies: A Tale of Babies, Vaccines and Deception* (2006).

Gary D. Kessler ("Death of the Second Frontier: Ode to America from Civil War to Moon Landing," poetry; "Last Treasures," nonfiction; "An Overview of Self-Review;" writing/publishing) is a former news agency managing editor, diplomat, newspaper columnist, theater critic, movie consultant, book editor, and publishing consultant. His published works include a short story collection, *On the Downtown Mall*; volume editor for the two-volume *WritersNet Anthology of Prose* and the four-volume *Blue Ridge Anthology*; coauthor of a publishing reference, *Finding Go! Matching Questions and Resources in Getting Published*; and a mystery novel, *What the Spider Saw.* He has won or placed in multiple Virginia Writers Club annual contests and the UVa Art Museum's Writer's Eye prose contest and took third place in the John Gresham–judged *The HooK* short story contest in 2011. A second short story collection, *Shadow of the Blue Ridge,* launched in the fall of 2015. His poetry has appeared in the *Piedmont Virginian*. He also writes pen name mystery novellas and novels.

Phyllis R. Koch-Sheras, PhD ("Crossing the Street: Connecting through Dream Work," nonfiction), is a clinical psychologist and author, living and working in Charlottesville since 1974. She has coauthored several books, including *The Dream Sourcebook*, *Couple Power Therapy: Building Commitment, Cooperation, Communication and Community in Relationships* and *Lifelong Love: Creating and Maintaining an Extraordinary Relationship*. Currently, she is writing a musical entitled "Therapy: the Musical." Phyllis is also a professional opera singer and watercolor artist. She has had several solo art exhibits in Charlottesville, which include poetry readings of her poems inspired by the paintings. She is married and has two grown children.

Martha Jean Lancaster ("The Warm Springs," nonfiction) is collections manager for The Fralin Museum of Art, University of Virginia. She is a Richmond native and descendant of French Huguenots and English who settled Virginia in the early seventeenth century. Ms. Lancaster has three stories published in *Skyline 2015*, launched at the Virginia Festival of Book. "Taking the Waters," about the historic Bath County pools, was published in *Skyline 2014*. Two essays are in the *Blue Ridge Anthology 2013*. Her nonfiction story, "Tantilla," won first place in the 2012 Blue Ridge Writers contest and second place in the Virginia Writers Club Golden Nib Contest.

Susan M. Lanterman ("The Time Capsule," nonfiction) writes human-interest stories for the "Commentary" section of Charlottesville's *The Daily Progress* newspaper, is writing a collection of short stories based on her Charlottesville B&B, and is concluding work on a young adult novel, "Hasta Luego, Santa Claus," which follows the antics of a teenager and his family of illegal immigrants.

Linda Levokove ("Chinese Food in Florence, Italy" and "A Spring Romance," poetry) is the author of two collections of poetry: *Walk On The Heart Side* and *Cabbages & Kings*. She is former vice president of the Blue Ridge Writers Chapter of the Virginia Writers Club and a member of the Poetry Society of Virginia and the Virginia Writers Club, which has presented her with a Special Award for Outstanding Service and Contribution to Poetry in Central Virginia. In addition, she has participated in The Charlottesville Festival of the Book, teaches a Poetry Critique Group at Olli/UVa, and has presented her poetry at several public venues. Presently Linda is working on a collection of poetry and short/short stories.

Sigrid Mirabella, ("Imagine War" and "Grass Vengeance," poetry) originally from Long Island, New York, defines herself as a social hermit and hopeful skeptic living in rural uncertainty. Her works have won awards and have appeared in *The Blue Ridge Anthology, Mid-America Poetry Review, Long Island Pet Gazette, Lynchburg News and Advance, Dog Fancy, Woman's Day, Countryside, People Magazines*, and various Macmillan/Howell books. In her other life, she works for a humane society in Nelson County, Virginia.

Brenda A. Morris ("Midnight," fiction; "Bound," nonfiction) is a retired teacher. She lives with her husband in Central Virginia. She began creating stories to tell her mother before she started school. Much of her writing is sparked by events that happened in her mother's or her past. Brenda writes short stories, memoirs, essays, and poetry.

Becky Mushko (*Skyline* spring contest nonfiction judge), retired Roanoke City teacher and 2006–7 writer-in-residence for Roanoke County Schools, currently serves as vice-president of both Lake Writers and the Franklin County Library Board of Trustees. She is a lifetime member of the Virginia Writers Club. She has self-published (*Patches on the Same Quilt*), vanity-published (*Peevish Advice, More Peevish Advice, The Girl Who Raced Mules & Other Stories, Where There's A Will*), small press-published (*Ferradiddledumday, Stuck*), online-published (her blog

Peevish Pen), and e-published. Her Kindle e-books are *Patches on the Same Quilt, Stuck, Over Coffee, Rest in Peace, The Best 'Un Yet, Miracle of the Concrete Jesus and Other Stories, Ferradiddledumday*, and *Little Meg Reddingoode*. Her stories have appeared in *A Cup of Comfort for Writers*, volumes II and III of the *Anthology of Appalachian Writers*, and many other publications. A three-time winner of the Sherwood Anderson Short Story Contest and five-time winner of the Lonesome Pine Short Story Contest, she is best known for her wins in the infamous Bulwer-Lytton Bad Fiction Contest—"Worst Western" (1998) and "Vile Pun" (2008). She blogs at http://peevishpen.blogspot.com; her Web site is http://www.beckymushko.com.

Deborah M. Prum ("Manners and Morals," fiction) is the author of *Fatty in the Back Seat* (a young adult novel), *First Kiss and Other Cautionary Tales* (an audiobook collection of humorous essays that first aired on NPR-member stations), *Czars and Czarinas* (an anecdotal and interactive history in iBook format) and *Rats, Bulls and Flying Machines* (a print book about the Renaissance). Her award-winning short fiction has been published in many places, including *The Virginia Quarterly Review, The Blue Ridge Anthology*, and *The Sweetbay Review*. Her humorous essays appear in many places, including the *Washington Post* and Charlottesville's *Daily Progress*, and air on NPR-member stations. Her work can be seen at www.deborahprum.com.

Elaine Ruggieri, ("Petite Small" and "Selective Memory" fiction) former vice president of public relations at the University of Virginia's Darden School of Business, has lived in Albemarle County since 1964. Having written nonfiction prose throughout her career, she is now concentrating on fiction. Her short story, "Deep Quarry," was published in *The Blue Ridge Anthology 2009*, "Doomsday" and the poem, "Lost in Verse," in *The Blue Ridge Anthology 2013*, "Playing Nightly," in *Skyline 2014*, and "Nun Run" in *Skyline 2015*.

Elizabeth Doyle Solomon ("Stella by Starlight," fiction: "Lesson from a Narcissus," poetry), a New Orleans native and retired teacher, began writing at age eleven and publishing at age thirteen. Now in her seventies, she reckons her poems total over 60,000. Elizabeth has published two poetry collections, *Seasons* and *The Steering Wheel Poems*, written newspaper columns, and founded the *Central Virginia Leader* newspaper. Her recent awards for both poetry and prose have come from the Poetry Society of Virginia and the Blue Ridge Writers and the *Skyline* anthology. She leads the Blue Ridge weekly poets' critique group, and her third book, *Journey West and Everywhere*, has been accepted for publication in 2016.

Olivia Stowe (*Skyline* volume editor; "Win Win" and "Clyde Saves Christmas," fiction) lives and writes in Central Virginia. Stowe's specialty is cozy mystery novellas, which include a thus-far ten-volume series of Charlotte Diamond mysteries, the most recent of which was *Fowler's Folly*. The Christmas-season short stories, "Cassandra's Last Spotlight" and "Blessedly Cursed Christmas," add to this series. She also is the author of the inspirational *Savannah* novella series. Stowe's standalone mysteries include *Fiddler's Rest*, *Restoration of the Castle*, and *Final Flight*. Her inspirational Christmas short story collections are available in the *Spirit of Christmas* and *Christmas Seconds* anthologies.

Jack Trammell ("Reflections on Running for Congress," nonfiction) lives on a farm in Central Virginia, where he is a modern agrarian and a recognized voice of Appalachia (born in Berea, Kentucky). His writing credits are diverse, ranging from hundreds of poems, articles, and stories to larger book-length projects and academic research related to his college teaching. He is a trained historian, a research methodologist, and an environmental advocate, but most of all he is committed to the act and art of writing, as well as encouraging others in their personal literary journeys. He can be reached at jacktrammell@yahoo.com.

Leonard Tuchyner ("April Mantis," poetry; "May Catfish and April Dog" and "A Passing World," nonfiction) is a semiretired counselor, living in Central Virginia with his wife and two dogs.

He maintains an active involvement in the local writing community, which includes participation in a writing critique group and in the Blue Ridge Writers Chapter of the Virginia Writers Club. Although challenged by legal blindness, he continues to pursue Tai Chi and related forms of martial arts. Gardening is another passion that has captivated him for most of his seventy-five-year life. One of his most fulfilling endeavors is the facilitation of a Senior Center's Writing for Healing and Growth writing group. He has been in the winners' circle of the Blue Ridge Writer Club's yearly writing contest several times. His winning entries have included poetry, fiction, and nonfiction. He has also been a regular contributor to *The Blue Ridge Anthology*. Mr. Tuchyner has published essays, poetry, and short stories in *Dialogue Magazine* (for which he is now a columnist), *Magnets and Ladders*, *Nomad's Choir*, *Westward Quarterly*, and *Skyline 2014*. A poetry book, *A Journey to Elsewhere*, was published in 2014.

Erin Newton Wells ("A Slow Spring Music" and "The Truth," fiction; "Seed," "A Late Spring," and "Exposed," poetry; "Thin Places" and "The Rites of Spring," nonfiction) lives in Charlottesville, Virginia, where she is winding down a career of over thirty years of teaching studio art in an art school she established. She has been writing all her life and is now reentering this more actively and publicly. Her poetry, fiction, and nonfiction currently appear in regional anthologies and journals.

Lauvonda Lynn M. Young ("No Longer in the Race" and "Love Unconditional," poetry; "Murder Exposed," nonfiction), author of the poetry collection *Just A Woman*, writes in various genres, including poetry, fiction, nonfiction, and memoir (mostly fact based). She has been published in anthologies, newspapers, magazines, and other sources. Lynn plans, organizes, moderates, and presents programs and workshops. She is a member of the Executive Committee of Poetry Virginia (Poetry Society of Virginia); she served as the program chair of the PV Annual Poetry Contest (2014); and is the chair for 2016. Past president of the Blue Ridge Writers Chapter,

Virginia Writers Club, Lynn received the VWC Superior Service Award in 2011. She holds memberships in the Appalachian Authors Guild (VWC), Blue Ridge Writers (VWC), Poetry Virginia (PSV), Virginia Writers Club, and WriterHouse.

Skyline 2015

The second collection of works by Central Virginia Writers.

Skyline 2015

Olivia Stowe, ed.

*Prose and Poetry
by Central Virginia Writers*

Skyline 2014

The first collection of works by
Central Virginia Writers.